YOUTH CULTUF
IN CHINA

China Today series

YOUTH CULTURES IN CHINA

Jeroen de Kloet and Anthony Y. H. Fung

polity

First published in 2017 by Polity Press

Polity Press
65 Bridge Street
Cambridge CB2 1UR, UK

Polity Press
350 Main Street
Malden, MA 02148, USA

ISBN-13: 978-0-7456-7917-4
ISBN-13: 978-0-7456-7918-1(pb)

A catalogue record for this book is available from the British Library.

Library of Congress Cataloging-in-Publication Data

Names: Kloet, Jeroen de, author. | Fung, Anthony Y. H., author.
Title: Youth cultures in China / Jeroen de Kloet, Anthony Y. H. Fung.
Description: Malden, MA : Polity Press, 2016. | Includes bibliographical references and index.
Identifiers: LCCN 2016016606 (print) | LCCN 2016018350 (ebook) | ISBN 9780745679174 (hardback) | ISBN 9780745679181 (pbk.) | ISBN 9781509512973 (Mobi) | ISBN 9781509512980 (Epub)
Subjects: LCSH: Youth–China–Attitudes. | Youth–China–Social conditions–21st century. | Culture–21st century.
Classification: LCC HQ799.C55 K56 2016 (print) | LCC HQ799.C55 (ebook) | DDC 305.230951–dc23
LC record available at https://lccn.loc.gov/2016016606

Typeset in 11.5 on 15 pt Adobe Jenson Pro
by Toppan Best-set Premedia Limited
Printed and bound in Great Britain by Clays Ltd, St. Ives PLC

For further information on Polity, visit our website: politybooks.com

Contents

Figures, Tables, and Images

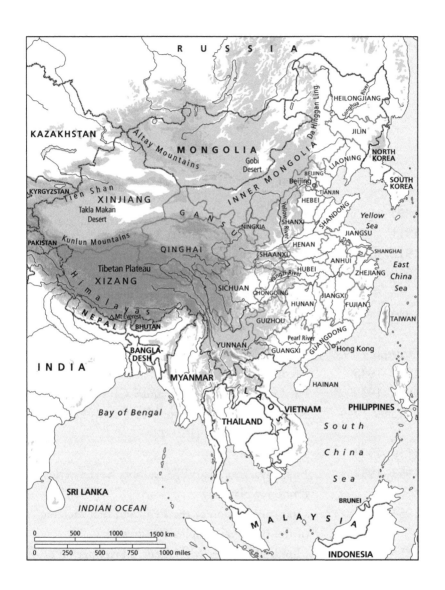

Chronology

1894–1895	First Sino-Japanese War
1911	Fall of the Qing Dynasty
1912	Republic of China established under Sun Yat-sen
1927	Split between Nationalists (KMT) and Communists (CCP); civil war begins
1934–1935	CCP under Mao Zedong evades KMT in Long March
December 1937	Nanjing Massacre
1937–1945	Second Sino-Japanese War
1945–1949	Civil war between KMT and CCP resumes
October 1949	KMT retreats to Taiwan; Mao founds People's Republic of China (PRC)
1950–1953	Korean War
1953–1957	First Five-Year Plan; PRC adopts Soviet-style economic planning
1954	First constitution of the PRC and first meeting of the National People's Congress
1956–1957	Hundred Flowers Movement, a brief period of open political debate
1957	Anti-Rightist Movement
1958–1960	Great Leap Forward, an effort to transform China through rapid industrialization and collectivization

March 1959	Tibetan Uprising in Lhasa; Dalai Lama flees to India
1959–1961	Three Hard Years, widespread famine with tens of millions of deaths
1960	Sino-Soviet split
1962	Sino-Indian War
October 1964	First PRC atomic bomb detonation
1966–1976	Great Proletarian Cultural Revolution; Mao reasserts power
February 1972	President Richard Nixon visits China; "Shanghai Communiqué" pledges to normalize US–China relations
September 1976	Death of Mao Zedong
October 1976	Ultra-leftist Gang of Four arrested and sentenced
December 1978	Deng Xiaoping assumes power; launches Four Modernizations and economic reforms
1978	One child family planning policy introduced
1979	US and China establish formal diplomatic ties; Deng Xiaoping visits Washington
1979	PRC invades Vietnam
1982	Census reports PRC population at more than one billion
December 1984	Margaret Thatcher co-signs Sino-British Joint Declaration agreeing to return Hong Kong to China in 1997
1989	Tiananmen Square protests culminate in June 4 military crackdown
1992	Deng Xiaoping's Southern Inspection Tour re-energizes economic reforms
1993–2002	Jiang Zemin is President of PRC, continues economic growth agenda

1997	Transfer of sovereignty of Hong Kong from the United Kingdom to the People's Republic of China
1999	Transfer of sovereignty of Macau from Portugal to the People's Republic of China
November 2001	WTO accepts China as member
2002–2012	Hu Jintao, General-Secretary of the CCP (and President of PRC from 2003)
2002–2003	SARS outbreak concentrated in PRC and Hong Kong
2006	PRC supplants US as largest CO_2 emitter
August 2008	Summer Olympic Games in Beijing
2010	Shanghai World Exposition
2012	Xi Jinping appointed General-Secretary of the CCP (and President of PRC from 2013)

Acknowledgments

Writing a book together in different parts of the world is a quite bewildering experience. However odd it may sound, the authors first and foremost would like to thank one another for this unique cooperation and joint effort, one that cheerfully strengthened our friendship. Throughout the writing process, we received actual and emotional support from numerous people. We thank the young people who so kindly made time to talk to us, and the fans, artists, musicians, game designers, television producers, and other media producers, who shared their thoughts, opinions and cultural practices with us. They, and the works they produce, make us want to return to China time and again.

It requires more than just two people to write such a book, and we turned to many more friends for ideas and inspiration. For this, we thank Florence Graezer Bideau, Daisy Cheng, Carlos Cheung, Matthew Chew, Gladys Pak Lei Chong, José van Dijck, John Nguyet Erni, Feng Jiangzhou, Jeroen Groenewegen-Lau, Jaap Kooijman, Eloe Kingma, Giselinde Kuipers, Stefan Landsberger, Jenny Lau, Song Hwee Lim, Christoph Lindner, Li Hao, Liu Jun, Lo Yin Shan, Sylvie Luk, Kevin May, Esther Peeren, Patricia Pisters, Thomas Poell, Boris Pun, Qin Liwen, Lena Scheen, Leonie Schmidt, Shum Si, Jan Teurlings, Brian Yeung, Frances Yeung, Zeng Guohua, Zhang Wuyi, Zhang Xiaoxiao, Zhi Tingrong, Zhou Xinping and Zuoxiao Zuzhou. Special thanks are given to Yiu Fai Chow for his encouragement and care. We also want to thank our family members for their support while we were occupied with fieldwork in Beijing, Shanghai, Guangzhou, Changsha,

Wuhan, and Shenzhen. We also want to express our gratitude to Emma Longstaff and Jonathan Skerrett from Polity for their trust, support, and patience. Ian Tuttle was of invaluable help in language editing. We would also like to thank the two anonymous reviewers for their supportive and critical comments and feedback. We are grateful to Shen Lihui, Zhang Xiaozhou, Wutiaoren, New Pants and Modernsky Entertainment Co. Ltd. for their permission to reprint lyrics. Iris Guan, Penn Ip, Pei Randi, and Irena Villaescusa helped a lot with data collection and archiving. Finally, we thank our students – BA, MA, and PhD – for their constant critical feedback, their questioning, and their curiosity.

This book uses multiple sources of data from different funded research projects, for which we are very grateful. For Anthony Fung, the funding source came from a research grant on gaming industries given by the Research Grant Council of HKSAR (Project no. 4001-SPPR-09) and a research grant about the comics industry from the Research Grant Council of HKSAR (RGC Ref no. CUHK14402914). Anthony Fung is also indebted to the support of his colleagues at the Chinese University of Hong Kong, School of Journalism and Communication at Jinan University where he is a Chair Professor, and School of Arts and Communication at Beijing Normal University where he serves as professor under the Global Talents Scheme. For Jeroen de Kloet, funding came from a VIDI grant from the Netherlands Organisation for Scientific Research on the cultural implications of the Beijing Olympics (NWO – Project no. 276-45-001), a Humanities in the European Research Area grant on single women in Delhi and Shanghai (12-HERA-JRP-CE-FP-586 SINGLE) and a consolidator grant from the European Research Council on creative cultures in China (ERC-2013-CoG 616882-ChinaCreative).

Introduction: Youth in China ————

Youth is always revolutionary
Revolution always belongs to youth.

Wen Yiduo (1899–1946)

I will keep on demanding freedom until you can't stand it. We need to keep on pushing; otherwise there will be no change.

Han Han (2012: 254)

Revolution is, and always should be, the characteristic of Chinese youth, as stated by the patriotic poet and democrat Wen Yiduo, who allied with the Communist Party to advocate for non-authoritarian rule by the ruling party Kuomintang of China in the 1940s. Revolution, for a long time, to be a taken-for-granted characteristic shared by this young generation, at least under the proletariat context in China. If we read the more recent musings of blogger, racing driver and cultural entrepreneur cum icon Han Han on his desire for freedom and change, it seems that this revolutionary zeal has not yet lost its glamour. But, as this book will show, his stance may be considered more as an exception to the rule, nor do the words we quote from him cover the whole spectrum, and above all the ambiguity, of his political and social critiques.

Indeed, what if, today, Chinese youth prefer to forsake revolution? Couldn't Chinese youth choose an easier, undemanding and more cool path as an alternative to outright rebellion? Should this be plausible, which we believe it is, then this book narrates a new Chinese revolution, not a Red Revolution nor the Long March of the Chinese Communist Party, but a whole brave new world in which Chinese youth eagerly abandon the baggage left by their political predecessors, discounting any unrealistic expectation imposed on them, and, maybe, abandoning pursuing ideals of freedom, democracy, and equality that many observers presume them to follow.

The questions that puzzle us are: what went wrong with the ideal of the communist doctrine and why are Chinese youth nowadays not as persistent as Wen Yiduo? Based on what we hear on Chinese media, and judging from Party practice, the answer may be quite simple. That is, the Party has flattened and controlled contradictions, and eliminated the tension between thesis and anti-thesis in history by whatever means that are commonly reported in international media, namely censorship, extortion, imprisonment, to name a few, thus ultimately creating a new China that does not entail revolution to begin with. It is an -ism that is neither communism nor socialism, perhaps an alternative historical trajectory no one has ever seen and a stage more advanced than that conceived by Karl Marx. What we are witnessing today is a China with a huge bureaucracy, a booming economy and an allegedly harmonious society highly regulated by the Party and bounded by their doctrines. All these merely seem to render the revolutionary ideal nonsensical, anachronistic, and inapplicable to contemporary China.

A society devoid of revolution is not uncommon. Like most social and political systems in the United States and Europe, it takes multiple smaller internal "rows," including the Great Leap Forward, Cultural Revolution, Open Door policy, Tiananmen student protest, and so forth, to produce gradual change, rather than a full-blown revolution. With the current support of a bubbling economy, one that started to show signs of moderation in 2015, advanced technology of control, and manifold forms of political surveillance in China, it is not hard to imagine there must be other possible ways for change. For researchers, rather than thinking in terms of revolution and democratization, it is important to follow the young generations and the intricate ways in which they navigate through different modes of culture that could accommodate, hinder, or embrace change, creativity, and ideals.

This book builds largely on two different sets of primary sources. First, we draw on years of fieldwork, mainly interviews and ethnographic studies, in different cities in China, from Beijing and Shanghai to Guangzhou and Shenzhen. We have been living there, going out with young people, joining them at rock concerts, for strolls in the park, and to gatherings in restaurants. Our fieldwork covers a long period, from 1992 up to 2016, which allows us at times to reflect on the changes that have happened, but also, and often more importantly, the continuities. The latter, among which we can mention the doctrines of family, education, and state, are in our view important to stress in order to counter the pervasive narrative of change and newness that haunts reports on China. But our main focus in this book will be on the ten years from 2005 up to 2015.

Second, we will reflect on the media uses of youth as well as on the representations of youth in contemporary popular and digital culture in China, ranging from rock songs to blockbuster movies, and from talent shows on TV to online gaming. This betrays our background in media studies, and our contention that today, people, especially young people, do not live *with* media, but rather, they live *in* media, given the ubiquitous presence of media in our daily lives (Deuze 2012). While we draw less on secondary sources, that is, on reports on youth in Chinese media and academic culture, we do make use of predominantly Chinese studies to get a better grasp of their values, their media usage, and their aspirations. We also read these studies at a meta-level; they help us understand the discourses that proliferate around youth in China, most prominently the discourses of "youth as trouble" and "youth as hope." For example, as we will see in chapter 4, several studies related to sexuality discuss the importance of good and healthy sex education. But by and large, we are in this book committed to a more ethnographic and media-studies approach that engages with the complexities and ambiguities of everyday lived realities of young people in China.

We contend that to frame youth culture in China in terms of either resistance or compliance is far too simplistic. Youth culture in China is not about revolution nowadays, nor is it driven by notions of (Western) democracy, and while it is opening up to global culture and the Internet, this does not forebode political change. This book thus steers away from aligning youth to resistance only or exclusively; instead, we consider youth to be an important prism to analyze *what is going on* in China today (see Grossberg 2010), and we see them as being a reflection of, but also constitutive of, the changes taking place in China. But as we already observed earlier, it is not only about change. In line with Paul Clark's book on youth culture in China (2012), it is important to acknowledge continuities as well, some of which are connected to a Confucian history, others to the more recent communist past. For those readers who expect us to fantasize youth as if we consecrate resistance and subjectivity, this book may disappoint them. Our story of youth in China aims to avoid the deeply black and the clearly white; instead, we muddle through different shades of grey that together constitute youth cultures – in the plural, indeed – in China.

NO MORE REVOLUTION

In retrospect, in the throes of a period of debauchery, social upheaval, political volatility and imminent threats from without, as occurred in the May Fourth Movement in 1919 in which students protested against the Chinese government's feeble response to Japan and other imperialists, Chinese youth would demand a revolution. In fact, Mao Zedong himself also claimed that the May Fourth Movement spearheaded communist formation in China. This is, however, not today's China. Nowadays, China provides a relatively stable environment for the single child to grow up in. In general, they receive a good level of education as indicated by the high literacy rate of Chinese youth (over 99 percent in 2012 according to UNICEF figures). A large number of them manage to get a stable job, although there is now an unemployment rate of 15 percent (Sharma 2014), but for those who are unemployed, their family generally supports them. With all the family's or even two families' resources betting on one child, many urban children do not have to juggle their ideals with their basic livelihood.

Increasingly, the young are going abroad for their studies nowadays. As Pál Nyíri, Juan Zhang, and Merriden Varrall argue about the generation born after 1980:

> Their childhood and early youth was more significantly marked by the emergence of a culture of consumption than by political campaigns, and studying overseas was as much a means to social advancement in China in the context of a marketized education and a highly competitive job market as an opportunity to settle abroad. While these students do not necessarily come from backgrounds that are considered elite in China, the very fact that they are free, and can afford, to study abroad identifies them as beneficiaries of China's recent transformations. (2010: 51)

Many kids today are well-off and are claimed to be sometimes spoiled – being derogatively called "little emperors." Surely with variations in terms of wealth, by and large, this generation lives in a more sumptuous way than the previous one. Today's youth live in historical and economic conditions that are not equivalent to the chaos in early twentieth-century China and hardly comparable to the Cultural Revolution in the 1960s. As society is also improving in terms of economic prosperity, basic infrastructure, and quality of life – perhaps except for political freedom – it might be wishful thinking that Chinese youth would unflinchingly defy the regime. Furthermore, the rising power of China on the global scene feeds into a youthful nationalism that is driving a state of social stability and opportunities for career, money, and power. Over the past decade or so, the notion of "we the people" has been successfully replaced by that of "we Chinese," making nationalism an important glue that holds society together (Gries 2004).

This rise of nationalism follows on from a period during which Chinese youth eagerly absorbed cultural influences from the outside, be it Japan and Hong Kong or the United States. Zhang Zhen analyzes how, at the turn of the century, two different processes or, as she calls them, mantras, best capture the spirit of Chinese culture: "*xiahai* (plunging into the ocean), meaning going into the risky business world, and *yu shijie jiegui*, which literally means linking up with the [rail] tracks of the world" (2000: 93). In this book, we will analyze in particular the implications of youth linking up with the world – a process that has intensified deeply since the turn of the century.

Quite often in our direct interactions with youth, many would articulate the clichéd claim that "China has a huge population," implying that there must be social problems and there is no simple solution to directly and quickly solve the problem, and thus a powerful state is needed. Often, the Soviet Union serves as the constitutive outside in this narrative, a place that may have had a *perestroika*, but that now suffers from corruption and a lack of freedom. Besides, this generation may still have their ideals, even though they are not mapped onto a desire for revolution. As blogger Han Han explains (quoted in de Kloet 2010: 24–5):

> As the previous generation was always working for the revolution, people keep on arguing that our generation does not have any ideals. Sometimes you want to win a game, or buy a pair of sneakers, these are all ideals. There is no difference between these ideals. Sometimes I fall

in love with a girl, so I want to get her, this is also an ideal. An ideal is actually a thought that motivates you to do whatever it takes.

Youth's challenge to the authorities is delayed and withheld. The compliant behavior of Chinese youth is also caused by their upbringing and education, as we will show in chapter 1, often backed up in terms of traditional Chinese culture. The rise of nationalism as a unifying ideology is not to be explained only by the hollowing out of communism, but is also connected to what we like to call a "national complex" about a rising China. The characteristics of this complex, which operates like a superiority complex (Laqueur 1956: 8), produce a structure of feeling in which one generally overestimates one's own nation and subscribes to its noble intentions, accompanied by a lack of self-criticism. This structure of feeling is mapped onto a teleological discourse, in which China is framed as a country still in development. Consequently, youth rationalize in this way the temporal deficiencies and inefficiencies of their society, and adopt a mythical vision of the country that is supposed to be moving toward becoming a fully developed, prosperous place in the not too distant future. This helps to explain why they are more docile as well as tolerant about the social situation, and feel more complacent about the current status quo. They are also not easily agitated to participate in various social events challenging the authorities. Such a national complex, coupled with the factor of a rising China and the bubbling economy, gives no reason to challenge the status quo.

Youth might marvel at the courage and virtues of political dissidents, and sympathize with them, but they will most likely not partake in protests, disorder, and petitions. We are not suggesting that youth in China have no ideals. On the contrary, exposure to the global media culture and intensified travel worldwide does impact the new generation in China. In line with studies on youth in other places, we expect that also Chinese youth will often feel that they are marginalized and excluded, as well as undervalued and lacking a voice and presence in the post-industrial city (Dillabough and Kennelly 2010). But rather than moving from mere pursuit of economic prosperity to individual self-expression of freedom and autonomy in what has been termed the post-materialist society (Inglehart 1977), Chinese youth straddle between consumerism and nationalism, between embracing the global while celebrating the local. Against the background of a rising China, we witness youth volunteering to help the victims of the Sichuan earthquake in May 2008, soon after they cheer loudly in their celebration of the Beijing Olympics, and two years later, in 2010, they do so once again during the World Expo in front of the global media.

The interesting mix of having simultaneously a cosmopolitan outlook while expressing strong nationalistic sentiments – a mix de Jurriëns and de Kloet (2007) refer to as cosmopatriotism – produces strange anomalies. On one day, youth may protest against Japanese textbooks, while the next day, they may well queue in front of the Japanese embassy to obtain a study visa. In the already quoted study on nationalism expressed by overseas Chinese students during the Olympic torch relay of 2008, Nyíri et al. show how "young overseas nationalists, with their strongly transnational personal lives and media practices, carry the Chinese state with them and continue to inhabit it. (…) students use the official discourse of nationhood as just one element of a shared vernacular to reinforce a sense of community" (2010: 53–4). The Internet serves as a crucial tool in shaping nationalism, as it provides the overseas students with a direct link to the homeland, just as their actions travel back to the mainland and instigate new waves of national pride.

To return to the question of revolution, we at least do not see youth as the seeds of revolution. Even though they might not be satisfied with the status quo, changing society through a revolution is rarely considered an option. Rather than thinking in terms of revolution and radical change, in this book, we will analyze how youth intervene in city spaces, alter social norms, and explore the Internet. These interventions include body and gender politics as seen in films, cultural politics in urban space, discursive identifications through and in popular culture, or networked communicative formations in the virtual world, to name a few.

YOUTHSCAPES

But what constitutes youth? There is a danger in bracketing youth in fixed terms like age or ethnicity. There are youth from the nouveaux riches to the grassroots, from grassroots to young entrepreneurs, from Han Chinese to ethnic minorities. Our book does not necessarily cover all youth. One group that is absent in our study is that of youth belonging to the minorities of China. We do, however, aim to be inclusive by not only devoting chapters on the more "mainstream" urban and cosmopolitan youth, and examine how they create their own space in the increasingly complex Chinese society in the wake of a totalizing state, but also devote one chapter to migrant youth. We also decided not to include youth that choose to "bypass" or escape the system by studying and living abroad (see Nyíri et al. 2010). The young generations we describe all engage with the state, society, and family, as we will show in chapter 1. In the subsequent chapters, we show how they navigate through their lives and negotiate their subjectivity by means of creative engagement.

The youth generation analyzed in this book is not based on a strict age cohort or bio-genealogical approach. The latter results in the naming of specific generations, a common discourse in media and online blogs in China, referring to the post-80s (*balinghou*), post-90s (*jiulinghou*) and the millennium generation (*linglinghou*). According to official statistics from China in 2010, out of the 1.3 billion people in China, youth aged 15–24 represent over 113 million, and if we define youth as those between the age of 15–29, there are around

213 million (Quandl 2014). Such narrowly defining youth according to age or age cohort, and presenting it as if a specific decade produces specific shared identities, runs the danger of essentializing generations. In a study of the generation born in the 1990s, the informants themselves also question the label, for example Fu, born in 1990 and studying in Sheyang says (in Shen and Wang 2012: 7):

> I was born in 1990. My thoughts are very different from someone who was born in 1995 or 1993. And now there are all kinds of media and the Internet so people receive something very fast. You can't just use a label like *90hou* to cover all people. I even don't like the concept such as *80hou* or *90hou*. Because people are so different in these ten years. I always feel it's unsuitable to use a label to describe it.

While later in this chapter we will briefly map studies related to the different generations, in our view, youth in China can be better understood within a sociological framework of generation, in Mannheim's understanding (1952), that is, more in terms of a group that shares, incorporates, internalizes, and realizes a similar value system. But there are profound disjunctures here as well: the value system of migrant youth is not similar to that of their urban affluent peers. Hence, in addition to the sociological understanding of youth in terms of shared values, we also subscribe to a more anthropological approach in which the diversity and multiplicity of youth culture is foregrounded. As such, we straddle between similarity and difference, overlap and disjuncture, in our analyses.

We choose to dissect contemporary youth culture at specific conjunctures and attempt to explain youth through the lens of culture. We analyze how they are connected to politics and state, society and social norms, the city and technology, media and global culture, to name a few. What we espouse is the enquiry of an inconclusive, subtle, and sometimes fragmentary process of the formation of youth cultures in

China. This process requires youth's continuous participation in and challenge of the political, social, and economic structures that underpin the cultural domain. A concept that gestures toward our approach is that of youthscape. This concept can be traced back to Appadurai's framework of appending "-scapes" to major social domains, and more precisely to Maira and Soep's conceptualization (2004: xvii), in which they define youth as an achievement rather than a fixed category or a psychological stage of development from childhood to adulthood. By achievement, instead of assigning an ontological meaning to the term, the authors hint at a condition in which youth are being produced and constituted by different social institutions repeatedly in daily life in which youth are participating and engaging. The notion of "scape" helps to underline that these constitutive relationships "are not objectively given relations that look the same from every angle of vision but, rather, that they are deeply perspectival constructs, influenced by the historical, linguistic, and political situatedness of different sorts of actors" (Appadurai 1996: 33).

But who are these actors in China, what are the forces that constitute the youthscapes and their fluidity? In China, they are the state, society, social institutions, including the family, the media, the school, and the knowledge, rituals, and rules that they produce that play an important role in shaping the youthscape. To understand the way power operates through and between these actors, we employ a Foucauldian perspective in this book. While one may expect that power is merely exercised through a panoptic system of surveillance and control in China, we believe that power has changed its face over the past decade. Panoptic power is still at play, for example in the way the Internet is used to monitor citizens, but alongside such more direct modes of control, a more subtle, refined, and individualized mode of biopower has emerged. As Lisa Rofel describes in her *Desiring China*, the desiring subject is: "the individual who operates through sexual, material, and affective self-interest" (2007: 3). When Han Han writes, as we quoted earlier, that "An ideal is actually a thought that motivates you to do whatever it takes," he confuses idealism with desire. Openness, flexibility, and self-development are all tropes that help constitute the modern Chinese youngster, and these tropes are implicated in discourses of neoliberalism that are mobilized by the nation-state (Ong 2006). The discourses Chinese youth create to redefine themselves may hold the power for change, yet this change may very well be the desired outcome and uphold the current status quo. What matters is when, where, and how subject positions are explored that may unsettle this harmony, and that may move beyond the templates as produced by the state, the school, the family, and the workplace.

According to one of the earliest and most prominent researchers on Chinese youth culture, Stanley Rosen, today's youth are living under competing and contradictory influences that shape their attitudes and values, in his words:

> They have become very *internationalist* in their outlook, and they are strongly affected by global trends. Likewise, they are very *pragmatic* and *materialistic*, largely concerned with living the good life and making money. The third competing influence, most often called *nationalism* in its more extreme form, represents a broader impulse and encompasses not only the defense of China against perceived enemies from abroad, but also the kind of love of country and self-sacrifice in support of those most in need that was evident in the volunteerism that followed the earthquake. (Rosen 2009: 361, original emphasis)

To grasp these complexities and contradictions, we argue that it is important to avoid generalizations, as well as clear and fixed definitions of what youth is and is not.

Thus, this book is not an official version of what youth are. In China, there are a vast number of experts that attempt to define, describe, and prescribe what Chinese youth are. These include the China Youth and Children Research Association (CYCRA, established in 1999) under the Secretariat Office of the Communist Party, China Youth Development Service Centre (founded in 1998) under the China Youth Pioneer National Youth Committee, Chinese Youth Development Foundation (CYDF, founded in 1989) and the China Youth and Children Research Centre (CYCRC) set up under the Youth Communist Party. The CYCRC, in particular, publishes annually official Trends of Chinese Youth Development Report (aka Youth Greenbook), Chinese Delinquency Annual Studies Report (aka Youth Redbook), and Political Attitudes of Chinese Youth Annual Studies Report, and book series such as Youth Research and Youth Movement History. Reading all these will suffice to know the official views on youth.

As one can imagine, these official records first define youth by age brackets. And after the biologically defined discourse, then youth are likely to be described from two angles: first, youth as naïve, vulnerable, and a problem, and, second, youth as hope for the future. This is not specific to China; also in other cultural contexts these are the two main discourses, with youth serving as a kind of "metaphorical vehicle" on which general hopes and fears are projected by society (Osgerby 2004). From the angle of adults, youth will be said to be the vulnerable and powerless cohort of society. In the eyes of adults, they are also defined as the unproductive group in society, and often regarded as indolent if they do not have any achievements to show. When youth actively demand their rights, proclaim their autonomy, or even fight for a higher goal in society, youth are considered a contentious or rebellious group. Reports from the youth association under the state for united propaganda frame youth in China as the future of China: for the sake of the country, they adhere faithfully to the Party's and leaders' ideology, participating in various charity work and contributing to the future and unity of society. It is here that the earthquake of 2008 helped support such state narratives: it showed how the young generation cared for

their country and its people, and how altruistic they could be, countering the narratives that claim they are selfish and materialistic. This
presents a quite one-sided and idealized version of what is going on.
All these publications give a top-down view and opinions on youth as
if they are subordinated under the regime of adults and the authorities.
However, in daily life, Chinese youth will feel uneasy with such official
notions that define them either as trouble or as hope. They struggle to
negotiate other possible subject positions, neither that of troublemaker
nor that of hope for the country – and it is these struggles that we
hope to unravel in this book.

As Alex Cockain writes in his book on urban youth in China, in
which he also makes a plea for a more nuanced understanding of youth
that resists easy binaries and easy generalizations:

> There has been a paradigm shift whereby young Chinese have shifted
> from being considered as group-focused, passive (easily manipulated),
> and politically oriented, brought up in times of scarcity and suffering,
> to individualistic, reflexive (less easily manipulated), a-political and con-
> sumption focused, with experiences of being brought up in times of
> abundance and excess. (2012: 8)

While we do observe such a shift, this change is far from unidirectional
or absolute. Like Cockain, we want to avoid reading Chinese youth
according to such simple frames. In this book, then, we are not going
to repeat the official prescription of youth culture in China – we aim
to steer away from univocal narratives that frame youth in terms of
either problem or hope. Nowadays, in China only a low percentage of
youth are actually active in the core establishment of the Communist
Youth League (CYL), established in 1922, the official recruiting wing
of the Chinese Communist Party. Based on a speech given at the 17th
National Congress of the CYL in June 2013, there are 89 million
members (Lu 2013), but this number is questionable. Less than half

of the members (49.9 percent) of the CYL are students, and during 2000–2005, on average only 160,000 students were absorbed into the Party annually (Xinhua 2007). In the past, kids were expected to serve as Red Guards for the Party during the Cultural Revolution. However, since the late 1990s, joining the Party is perceived as a possible benefit for job opportunities and establishing a network; often parents push their child to become a member. But only some "elite" youth can have the privilege of entering into the vested clique of the Party. As Rosen observes, "in a survey of more than 2,000 students from various universities in Xi'an, only 11.5 percent said that they wanted to join the Party because they believed in communism; other surveys and interviews have revealed that most applicants have little knowledge or even interest in most Party activities and goals" (Rosen 2009: 365).

Party membership thus is no longer a strong dividing principle, and many people we talked to claim with a smile full of irony that they are Party members, clearly distancing themselves from the possible communist associations. Nationalism seems to have replaced communism as a possible binding ideology, but even this may operate as a contradictory and quite shallow set of values. As Rosen remarks correctly:

> even those youth who felt they had to "show patriotism" by honouring the short-lived attempt to boycott Carrefour, the French superstore, in response to French interference with the Olympic torch relay during its Paris run, made sure to use up all their discount coupons and finish their shopping prior to the May 1 boycott. (2009: 363)

Nationalism is thus only one of the possible subject positions youth experiment with, alongside other subject positions. In this creative play they draw on numerous resources, multiple scripts of reality, derived from their direct surroundings, but also from the Internet and other media, like film, television and music. What matters then is to map out these different scripts, and probe into the creative appropriations as mobilized by today's youth.

Rather than reading youth culture in terms of anti-hegemonic struggle, we prefer to think of youth as experimenting with different cultural repertoires. This differs from a subcultural approach in which youth is mainly read in terms of resistance and rebellion (Hebdige 1979). Especially the urban, educated youth are being fostered by the system and are acquiring a relatively advantageous position, at least in terms of social resources that they can command and maneuver. They choose a balanced mode of survival and experiment with exploring different cultural alternatives.

CHANGING YOUTH VALUES

Studies in and outside China show how the values of Chinese youth have been changing over the past decades. To probe their political values, we draw on a 2015 study from the Chinese Academy of Social Sciences that is based on a large sample of 10,206 respondents born between the 1940s and the 1990s. Figure 0.1 presents the political engagement of the different generations.

Contrary to what might be expected, we witness a steady rising interest and involvement in politics in this study: younger people talk more about it, they discuss politics on the Internet, and while few took part in a demonstration or strike, many would like to. The title of the study, "Is the silent revolution coming?" hints at the possibility that underneath the image of a compliant generation, something more rebellious may be rising. We may wonder, however, if the observed political zeal is not more related to age than to generation – that is, the older people get, the less politically engaged they become. This corresponds with life-cycle theory that posits that "each young group that enters the population starts with more modern attitudes and becomes steadily more traditional as it ages" (Shi 2015: 91).

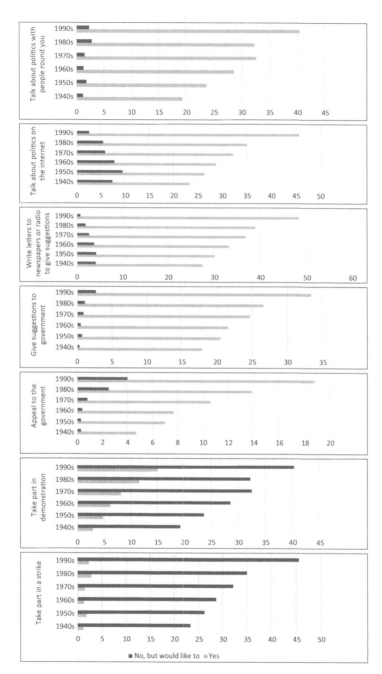

Figure 0.1. Public participation of different generations
Source: C. Li 2015: 103

Table 0.1. Comparison of democracy consciousness between generations

To what extent do you agree with the following sentences?		1940s	1950s	1960s	1970s	1980s	1990s
The government takes care of state affairs, ordinary people should not take care of it	Yes, I agree	50.7	48.8	44.3	33.1	24.5	12.7
	No, I don't agree	49.3	51.2	55.7	66.9	75.5	87.3
Ordinary people should listen to the government, subordinates should listen to the superior	Yes, I agree	70.4	68.1	62.1	50.3	41.6	29.3
	No, I don't agree	29.6	31.9	37.9	49.7	58.4	70.7

Source: C. Li 2015: 103

In the same study, questions were asked about whether the government should be allowed control over the people (table 0.1). These figures present an increasing mistrust in the authority of the Party, or, what may be more fair to say, a questioning of hierarchy. The younger the generation, the stronger the democracy consciousness (C. Li 2015: 104). The author of the study concludes that there is a shift from values pertaining to materialism towards post-material values for the younger generations (C. Li 2015: 104). Rather than reading these statistics as a sign of an upcoming revolution, it makes more sense in our view to interpret them as pointing toward the increased independence and individualism of the younger generations. As we argue throughout this book, this individualism does not necessarily imply more freedom. The figures focus solely on political statements, taking a quantitative approach. However, the possibility to strike, to demonstrate, to protest remains highly limited in China, and in our view the cultural spaces that we describe in this book may offer safer and therefore more popular avenues for exploring different subjectivities.

As we will show in chapter 1, when we discuss further the role of the Party in everyday life, other studies show that support for the state remains strong. In addition, figures on media use of Chinese youth attest to the importance of entertainment, more so than politics. A study by Tencent – a leading Internet company in China – among 8,041 respondents from youth born in the 1990s shows that 56.1 percent focus on entertainment news, 40.2 percent on technology news, 32.4 percent on society news, 27.0 percent on politics and 24.5 percent on cultural issues. Popular culture and entertainment thus rank highest among the news interests of Chinese youth, according to this survey (Yiguanzhiku and Tengxun 2014: 23). This report also rather contradicts the earlier study, as in the Tencent study, when compared to those born in the 1990s, the generation born in the 1980s shows a stronger interest in society and law, while the younger generation has more interest in entertainment and technology (Yiguanzhiku and Tengxun 2014: 24). Studies of the 1990s generation all point to their increased reliance on themselves. The Tencent study quotes, for example, 18-year-old Yu, a college student, who says:

> When we need to choose between liberal arts direction and science direction in high school, my grades on both sides were nearly the same. My parents wanted me to choose science very much because it's easy to find a job. But I was determined to choose the arts direction in which I was more interested. When I need to choose a major for college, they wanted me to choose economy or finance, but I remained committed to my own interest and chose journalism. To be a reporter is my dream. My own path should certainly be chosen by myself. (Yiguanzhiku and Tengxun 2014: 11)

As we will show throughout this book, such a narrative of self-determination is fraught with contradictions and inconsistencies. The demands to get a good job, lead a healthy life, get into a stable relationship, take care of one's parents, to name but a few, are both enabling as well as limiting. On top of that is the real-estate boom, or bubble, that makes it nearly impossible to buy a house. One study quotes Song, a student from Chengdu:

> I really can't accept the house price rising. Housing is beating this generation down. The 80s generation all say that they are the generation that is beaten down by the price of houses. (Shen and Wang 2012: 187)

By and large, the often heard critique in China toward Chinese youth as being materialistic and selfish is debunked by these studies. The same study, which focuses on the digital life of those born in the 1990s, writes that:

> In society, people would say 90hou is the "beat generation" (*kuadiaodeyidai*) or the "decadent generation" (*tuifeideyidai*). After our survey, it is found that reality is different. According to the result of 1600 questionnaires, 77.8% students claim "I would work hard for my dream." 54.6% claim "I have a relatively clear plan for my college life." Only 22% claim "I feel very confused about my future." (Shen and Wang 2012: 23)

Nevertheless, the pressure in life is increasing: one study showed that, in 1998, 23.1 percent of the respondents felt pressured and depressed, while this figure rose to 55.1 percent in 2008 (Lin 2008: 18). Another study comparing youth born in the 1980s with those born in the 1990s shows that when asked what quality they feel they need the most, among the qualities listed, the one that increased the most was competitiveness, which rose from 45.4 percent to 70.6 percent (Zou 2011: 72). These studies offer some glimpses of the changing values of

Chinese youth. At the same time, they run the danger of producing cohorts based on decades that tend to ignore differences and multiplicities. The studies serve in this book as a background setting; they show the fallacies of portraying Chinese youth as lacking in values or being overtly materialistic.

THE CHAPTERS

The constant stress on multiplicity constitutes the main argument of this book. This is, we agree, a rather basic and rudimentary argument, namely, just as one cannot claim China to be one entity, and just as Chineseness is fraught with contradictions and contestations, so it is impossible to think and write of Chinese youth as if it were a singular category. Our book sets out to empirically undermine any generalizing claim about youth in China. In a time when media constantly write of the rise of China, such questioning of China's singularity remains urgent. This argument also allows us to engage with a wide array of cases, ranging from migrant youth to *Weibo* activism.

Youth in China are not actively pursuing democracy, as their counterparts did in Hong Kong in the fall of 2014, nor do they aim to topple the system, as was the case in the Arab Spring, nor do they publicly fight against corruption, as their predecessors did in 1989. They are indeed quite different from the generation that grew up in the 1980s, the decade during which a cultural fever swept over China that mesmerized the young, who, in their search for a different meaning of life, looked elsewhere, beyond the border of China, toward the West (for an analysis of youth culture in the 1980s, see Xu 2002). Instead, today's youth are in search of small interventions, piecemeal changes, occasional resistance and locally specific alternative subjectivities. But, as we will show in chapter 1, there are clearly limitations in this search for and experimentation with different cultural trajectories and subjectivities. Youth have little control or voice in the formal domains of education, family, and the state. On the contrary, these are the domains that frame youth in either the overtly negative image of problematic and lacking in quality (*suzhi*), or its inverse frame, in which they are the hope for an even more prosperous future. While we will show in this chapter how these discourses are quite persistent over the past decades, we refrain from giving a comprehensive historical analysis of youth culture. For a more thorough genealogy of the transformation of youth from Red Guards in the 1960s into political protesters in the 1980s toward today's globally connected youth, we refer the reader to Clark (2012), Cockain (2012), and Xu (2002), and for a study of youth during the 1990s, please refer to Jeroen de Kloet's *China with a Cut* (2010).

In the remaining chapters, we are interested in the creative cultural repertoires youth mobilize to navigate the demands imposed upon them and their own aspirations. These involve creative strategies, alternatives that are often elusive, sporadic, and ad hoc – which also involves a negotiation between youth and the different authorities. This echoes with other analyses of youth (e.g., Warikoo 2014), which argue that the seemingly oppositional styles, tastes in music, and school behavior is the result of a balance between youth's entanglement with their peers and their alliance with formal authorities.

The immediate space that youth engage with is leisure and entertainment. Media, popular culture, arts, and other visual cultures that youth are exposed to in their everyday lives constitute a platform of signs, symbols, and images that youth appropriate so as to negotiate their subjectivities (Carey 1989). These feed into an "individualizing, consumption-oriented, urban and technologically-mutable" Chinese society in which a socialist market economy, cultural globalization, and strong authoritarian Party ideologies are all at work (Wagner et al. 2014: 1). In chapter 2 we will show, through an analysis of the appropriation of global music styles, fashion styles, and digital styles, that they all operate as important domains through which Chinese youth experiment with different identities, different lifestyles, different embodiments. These can be politically sensitive styles, but when these are played out, it is mostly in a specific place at a specific moment. Chinese youth culture, as Paul Clark rightly observes, cannot be understood in simple binaries like "Chinese and Western, local and global, or traditional and modern. The developments were more complex and also spontaneous, ungoverned, uneven, and unpredictable" (2012: 192).

While we focus in chapter 2 on the localization and appropriation of what are perceived as Western cultural forms like rock music and fashion, in chapter 3 we turn to inter-Asian cultural flows, particularly from Japan and South Korea. Here, we engage more explicitly with practices of cultural translation, practices that in the case of mainland China often involve censorship and processes of Sinification. We look at how the drama series *Meteor Garden* in its Chinese version dilutes the issues of class differences and social inequality. The Korean reality gameshow *Running Man* also works hard to evade social issues, yet, precisely because of this apolitical nature, a lively youth culture has emerged around the show. We show how music stars and groups like *Super Girl* winner Li Yuchun, SNH48 and TFBoys all carve out a space for youth, sometimes critical, sometimes less so. These emerging cultural spaces so far remain by and large unnoticed as they are playful, digital, and seem innocent. But they do hold the potential for the formation of new youth subjectivities, thus further fragmenting the idea of youth in China.

In chapter 4 we analyze the links between youth and gender and sexuality. Starting with a brief history of gender and sexuality in China, we first map out the reification of heteronormative discourse through the lens of different academic studies as well as in media representations and cultural practices. Then we discuss three different angles that hold the power to unsettle heteronormative discourse in China: romance comedy, queer cultures, and sexuality and feminism. We analyze profound changes that allow for experimentations with new sexualities, new forms of dating, and new modes of relationship between same gender partners, changes in which new media, including advanced dating apps, often play a crucial enabling role. Having said that, we have also tried to caution against a too celebratory account: the detainment of five feminists in March 2015 as well as the censoring of the online gay series *Addiction* – cases we will further analyze in this chapter – attest to an increasingly strict environment. Furthermore, the desiring young self is, as we show in this chapter, implicated in different governmental power structures.

It is tempting to focus solely on the emerging hip urban lifestyles of youth in urban China. This would, however, ignore the vast number of young people in the countryside, especially those that move to the city and aspire to a new and more prosperous life. In chapter 5, we will reflect upon the life and struggles of migrant youth in China. We argue that in current debates, their identity as a migrant worker overshadows their youthfulness. In our view, it is important to zoom in on the link between both – which is what we do by analyzing the ways they use media, the ways they are represented in media and the ways they have become media producers themselves. We will, for example, show that migrant youths are intrigued by new media technology when they discover their potential and develop their own cultural practices to overcome various barriers to be integrated into the city. This turns out to be a recurring theme in our book: the importance of new technologies. Paul Clark (2012) espouses that today's availability of the Internet provides a space for youth to express their personal annoyance and disappointment about their society. In her study of urban Chinese youth, Liu Fengshu (2013) argues that the interaction between youth and the Internet holds the potential to effect, or at least contribute to, far-reaching economic, social, cultural, and political changes. This book investigates how youth and mobile communication technologies interact with each other to create new possibilities in a Chinese context.

CREATIVE WARFARE

The youth cultures we analyze through the lens of films, music, mobile technology, and global culture, all flourish inside mainstream popular culture. Youth's popular culture does not necessarily appeal to all audiences. And even the cultural forms that are highly popular across different age groups will differ in meaning for these respective groups. Youth culture is always implicated in the formal institutions, dominant culture, or hegemonic ideologies, and the construction and creation of youth culture is always connected to what official culture affords and enables. The development of youth culture in China, by and large devoid of a revolutionary zeal, foretells an often neglected view about Chinese youth. It may be more hopeful than we think; today's youth have the potential to promote change amidst continuity. This generation is quite different from the older generation that survived the Cultural Revolution. The latter often hold a cynical and gloomy view of the future of China. When the older generation looks at today's

Image 1. Romance at Tiananmen Square (photo by Jeroen de Kloet in 2008)

youth, with their history of tormented experience and unforgettable suffering, they either see youth's indulgence in popular culture, gaming, consumption, and sexuality as problematic, or they support them to excel and lead a prosperous life. In both cases, the older generation does not have much hope for China. Indeed, nowadays, rich Chinese families send their kids overseas for study and immigration simply because they have no hope for the future of China.

But the youth we interview say, "I think China will become better one day." Their way to respond to contemporary China is that they have created their own temporal youth culture, in which they mediate between idealism and reality. The temporality is also caused by the constant deterritorialization of youth in urban city settings (Auge 2009: 78; García-Canclini 1995: 229; Tomlinson 1999: 107; Zhang 2000), which refers to the weakening of relations of culture to the geographical and social territories. "Natural" and "organic" experiences of place, for example, of school and education grounds, or family homes, where youth could crystallize their identity, are continuously displaced, coerced, and arranged by the state as well as by the forces of globalization. These produce new spaces or transit points for youth that include shopping malls (which are more connected to capitalist consumption), pop concerts (for global consumption of pop music), or cybercafés, games, or the online world (which did not exist before). Fan communities subtitle the latest queer series from the West, like *Cucumber*, they are hooked on to the home-made online series, just as they also consume – playfully, good-humoredly, but also sarcastically – the popular online patriotic comic of 2012 *Those Years, those Rabbits and those Events* (*nalian nadu nasheshi*). Their ambiguous interpretations, readings, and sometimes creative digital appropriations, attest to our observation that youth culture now embraces not only ideals, values, and concerns; it also reflects the complex coexistence, predicament, and entanglement of nationalism, individualism, socialism, capitalism, and globalism.

Paraphrasing Umberto Eco (in Hebdige 1979), we could use the term "creative warfare" to describe how youth in China are able to construct a new mode of life within the context of a controlled and highly demanding life world with only limited resources. In terms of space, as mentioned earlier, youth basically do not own any space but they are able to "vernacularize" the state-coerced institutions, controlled spaces, and stern rules, and creatively bestow a unique meaning upon them, and at times challenge the status quo. What will come out of this creative warfare, we argue in the conclusion of this book, cannot be entirely anticipated. Creativity does not necessarily imply idealism or change, and why should it? It may, however, empower youth. We conclude the book by pointing at how youth engage in a politics of hope. China's evolving youth culture is inevitably polymorphous. Communication technologies push youth's opportunities to experiment with different cultural repertoires rendering any structural and ad hoc control of the state problematic if not meaningless. The everyday interactions and interpretations that are built on digital and popular culture such as music, writings, film texts and so forth, challenge the sanitized space and controlled organizations from the state. In China, popular youth culture constitutes a platform for fantasizing, aspiring, bypassing, or transcending politics. The cultural politics or creative warfare of youth may eventually make an impact on politics, but we just do not know when or where this will happen, and with what consequences. What we do hope to do is to reveal more of such glimpses in this book, on a par with examples of the continuous power of the nation-state.

To look at youth culture in this way, we can claim that youth culture in China is a paradoxical co-creation by youth and the state. Chinese youth are involved in a daily semiotic struggle over their spaces, their subjectivities, and their aspirations. But it is also a creation of the state because they formulate the rules, regulations, and modalities under which youthscapes proliferate. As Cockain argues, in China "young people feel most secure when control in their lives is combined with space for exploration and self-expression" (2012: 17). Between created and creating, between control and exploration, between biopolitics and technologies of the self, there are many possibilities. All depends on what the authorities want to create for youth, and subsequently, how youth themselves respond by re-creating their youthscapes. This may help to multiply the youthscapes, as our inquiries will show. There are many youth cultures just as that there are more Chinas. In a quite ironic way, our belief in the agencies, capacities, and intensities of today's youth somehow resemble that of Mao Zedong, who said:

The world is yours. It is also ours. But fundamentally, it is yours. You youngsters are energetic at the crack of dawn resembling the sun at 8 or 9am in the morning. We put our hopes in you.

1 Youth and Power: Education, Family, and the State

> When youth are strong, the nation is strong
> When youth move forward, the nation then moves forward.
>
> Liang Qichao (1873–1929)

INTRODUCTION

Liang Qichao was a Chinese philosopher, scholar, journalist, and a supporter of the most important student movement in the early decades of the twentieth century, the May Fourth Movement. His will to save the country was always no more than "self-strengthening," and according to his words, such seed should spark off from the youth. Given that Liang pushed in his writings for democracy in China, would he also advise youth to be the democratic pioneers in contemporary China? We would presume that if Liang were still alive, his call for democracy would not be answered by youth today, resonating with the same failure of his short-lived reform, the Hundred Days Reform during the late Qing Dynasty in the summer of 1898. If the monarchy or forces for the restoration of the monarchy were the major obstacles those days, what he would face nowadays would not just be the People's Liberation Army of the Communist Party. Rather than operating in such a top-down mode, power now traverses through every domain of society, including its institutions like school and the workplace, in everyday life and the desires for love, material well-being and success, as well as through and in the media. We witness a Foucauldian intensification of power: "power becomes lighter, more ubiquitous, less attached to 'negative' objects or practices (the disciplinary family, 'the father's no'), and more saturated within formerly ignored realms of social practice. In short, power becomes more effective while offering less obvious potential for resistance" (Nealon 2008: 71).

In the following chapters we are predominantly concerned with these intensifications of power in realms beyond the family and the state, in particular media, everyday life practices, and technologies of the self. In this chapter we engage with the strong ideologies in a triumvirate of institutions that span private and public domains in China, namely family, schooling, and politics. As Liu Fengshu remarks, the pressure for urban youth comes mainly "from high parental expectations typical of the only-child family, the exam-oriented educational system and fierce competition in society and the changed standard of a 'good life' " (Liu 2013: 89). In a study among students in Fujian, the respondents were asked what was most troublesome to them. Their top three resonate with the results of Liu's study: 50 percent replied they don't have a clear goal to fight for, 48.9 percent listed the difficulty of finding a job as a key problem, while 38.5 percent referred to study pressure (Lin 2008: 86).

The competition in society is, as we will show in this chapter, entangled with Party membership. To discuss familism, pedagogy, and partyism in this chapter helps us to understand the forces that bracket youth culture. With the ever (re)structuring society, economy, and politics, youth in urban China fall into the orbit of family in private life, school in public life, and politics in both domains. With only rare exceptions in rural areas, youth have been segregated from production and largely put under these systems to learn, reproduce, and practice the ideologies that they are being taught daily. From the discipline imposed upon them in the family to the textbooks of a school, they are all molded into subjectivities that prepare them not only for family life and life at school but also later in the society at large. In what can be seen as an increasingly value-vacuous society, the influence of the family has returned with a vengeance and it can be argued that it exerts an even stronger surveillance over the new generation given that the development of a single child in a typical family is being planned and prearranged by his or her family until, and even after, their marriage. The missed opportunities parents experienced because of the Cultural Revolution often amplifies their expectations toward the life of their only child – although again this will be different in rural areas and among minorities, where one can have more than one child. Politics, through the organs of the Communist Party, penetrates into school, community, workplace, and any listed institutions in society. As such, it infiltrates profoundly into the everyday life of Chinese youth, governing their life, career, and promotion chances.

In that sense, it is not accurate to read the family, the school, or the state as univocal disciplinary institutions that impose their views on youth. What we describe here echoes more Foucault's concept of governmentality, which is not only limited to the state's centralized control. It extends through various capillaries of social and cultural channels to manage political activities and events, family and household, and pedagogy and education. Governmentality here refers to the conduct of conduct, meaning that there exists knowledge or a set of rules in society that defines, restricts, and normalizes norms, practices, obligations, responsibilities, and disciplines of an individual, a family, or an organization (Lemke 2002). We seldom talk about top-down power at this point, not because there is no power and coercion in the hierarchical society in China. Instead, we adopt a framework of governmentality to understand the relationship between government and its governance and the everyday management of citizenship, desires, labor (as illustrated in chapter 5), sex and gender identity (as illustrated in chapter 4) by examining imported global and popular culture (as illustrated in chapters 2 and 3), discourse on social media, marriage, and rituals, respectively (e.g. Jeffreys and Sigley 2009). The power exercised toward others with the intention to maintain order limits the behavioral range of possibilities for youth. The concept of governmentality here articulates power with political knowledge as well as discovers and regurgitates the rationality based on which such power is exercised spontaneously (Foucault 1981). In daily life, thus we can see that youth, parents, teachers, and social institutions in various domains all follow various practices and values that more or less reflect the systematized telos or reasoning of actions. These values and practices can be readily read in youth's daily lives, from family interactions, learning and schooling, and job employment, to name a few.

POLITICAL VALUES AND PARTY MEMBERSHIP

To what extent do Chinese youth support the China Dream of Xi Jinping? The study we quoted in the previous chapter comparing different generations gestured to an increasingly critical attitude toward the authorities. But other studies show at the same time a strong support for China's current path. In a comparative study between the generations born in the 1980s (sample of 800, taken in 2004) and 1990s (sample of 1200, taken in 2009), 47.0 percent of the 1980s generation and 45.5 percent of the 1990s generation would agree with the statement that "socialism will beat capitalism," while 41.6 percent and 50.1 percent respectively agree with the statement that "socialism and capitalism will gradually be the same." Interestingly, while from the 1980s generation 58.8 percent think that until the middle of the twenty-first century China will be a socialist country led by the CCP, among the 1990s generation this figure is even higher: 79.0 percent (Zou 2011: 71–2). This increase in support may also be due to the timing of the two surveys, in 2009, just after the Beijing Olympics, more youth may be in support of the system than five years before that.

A study among college students, published in China in 2013 and based on a sample of 6727 surveys in 19 different colleges in China, shows how much the respondents continue to support the Party line. For example, 42.9 percent claim to be very confident in China's rejuvenation in the twenty-first century, and 49.7 percent are confident, only 7.4 percent are less confident or not confident at all (Shi 2013: 24). When comparing this confidence between Party members, Communist Youth League members, and non-members, however, there is quite a striking difference; while from the former two categories only 5.3 percent and 6.8 percent do not feel confident about China's rejuvenation, among the non-members, this figure is clearly higher: 33.4 percent. The figures for confidence in the future development of the socialist road with Chinese characteristics are quite similar; while only 6.1 percent of the Party members and 11.4 percent of the Communist Youth League members lack confidence, among non-members this figure is much higher: 40 percent. However, the figures on which this comparison is based are skewed: at college, most students are members of either the Party or the Youth League. In this sample, 28.4 percent are CCP members, 68.2 percent are members of the Youth League, and only 3.4 percent are non-members (Shi 2013: 26–7). We combined some of the most interesting figures pertaining to political values from this book-length study in table 1.1. Also here there are stark differences between the very small portion of non-members, and the much larger number of Party members in the sample, with the former being less inclined to toe the Party line. These figures suggest quite solid support for the authorities, but the reasons for joining the Party may be much more pragmatic, rather than ideological.

Looking for a job is a major challenge for Chinese youth nowadays. China does not release youth unemployment figures, but there are reasons to believe they are high. The first and the largest-scale study "China's First Youth Employment Condition Survey Report," jointly released in 2005 by the official All-China Youth Federation (ACYF)

Table 1.1. Political values of Chinese college students

	COMPLETELY AGREE	AGREE	DISAGREE	CAN'T SAY
Marxism has strong and durable vitality	48.3	39.8	4.6	7.3
China can't use the Western multiparty system	39.6	35.1	17.4	7.9
The direction and path of Chinese reform and opening up is completely right	41.4	45.2	7.8	5.6
The guiding ideology of the country can't be diversified	32.4	34.3	24.6	8.7
Separation of the three powers is the best polity of modern country governance	17.1	30.1	30.8	22
Privatization is the only way for developing countries to become prosperous	32.4	34.3	24.6	8.7

Source: Shi 2013: 31–5

and Institute of Human Resources and Society Security (ISS) (Dai 2005), already indicated that the unemployment rate had reached 15 percent for those under the age of 21. Given that the working population increases by 20 million annually and that there are only 10–16 million available jobs, youth's job search is expected to be an uphill struggle. In 2014, CNBC figures indicated that the youth unemployment rate had reached 9.6 percent (Tao 2014). Given that China is the nation with the highest economic growth rate, a rate that started to falter in the year 2015 however, it is indeed a very high figure. Yet, the new generation has to survive. The cracks in the rice bowl of Chinese youth (Zhang 2000), a result of the dismantling of social security in post-Deng China, result in an increasingly precarious future for Chinese youth, characterized by less and less security in terms of income and job status. Graduating from Tsinghua and Peking University and even from elite universities overseas might secure a job in international companies. For those who are less lucky – and they are the majority – searching for a stable occupation in the huge field of government offices or related organizations is perhaps the second best strategy. As the Party system operates in parallel with the government, a Party member in many ways has advantages over non-members. To be a Party member is an advantage when applying for jobs, especially in public positions. Thus, partyism is also becoming a religion in a secular sense: it is not just subscribing to a belief; being a Party member gives certain groups of people a strategic advantage in securing a job, and also a sense of pride, especially during a time when the Communist Party is steering the nation to become a world political and economic center of power. To the end of 2014, official figures indicated that the number of Communist Party members had reached 87.8 million, and the number of members aged under 35 was 22.5 million, constituting 25.6 percent (Renminwang 2015). Over the years, the number of Party members has increased: in 2007, 73.4 million Chinese were Party members, 6.4 million more than the number in 2002. In 2007, 17.4

Image 2. State presence at the 2012 Strawberry Music Festival (photo by Jeroen de Kloet)

million of them (23.7 percent) were aged under 35 (gov.cn 2007). These figures show how more, rather than fewer, Chinese opt to become a Party member, but in total, approximately only 6.4 percent of the population are members.

Partyism here refers to the tendency toward an active participation and organization of political parties under a political system. Of course, under the PRC, it refers to a uni-partyism concept that we use to describe the inseparability of youth, school, and work with the Party. In school, the Party secretary rules in conjunction with the Principal in high school and the President in university, respectively. There are also youth partisan leaders in each class. This system is designed as a control mechanism to discipline the alternative voices and to mainstream Party ideology. However, political as it is, its perceived function changes in the eyes of youth. While a youth member has to attend regular meetings to plead loyalty, receive Party education, and report "irregularities" among their cohorts, these obligations are also exchanged with concrete and tangible rewards and privileges in different settings.

A particularly salient example comes from the Party's role in the workplace. Communist Party membership these days in China is important in particular to secure a leadership position in a public institution. But it is also a point of contention; no youth would be willing to utter his or her views about the Party in public. If youth were asked whether they would like to join the Party, they would probably keep their mouth shut or respond in an ambiguous manner for various reasons. A member we interviewed told us implicitly that because Communist members in the peer's community might still carry negative connotations such as dictatorship or corruption, she tried not to publicly declare that she was a Party member. Quite obviously, Chinese youth want to evade discrimination from those that share an undesirable attitude toward the Party.

Admittedly nowadays, having reached out to the world through the Internet and the influx of global culture into China, Party members might not openly justify the various practices of the Party, including issues of freedom, human rights and bureaucracy, but they would not defy Party rules or discredit Party ideologies either. Resonating with the beliefs of many Chinese, for the new generation, there is a discrepancy between what the Communist Party advocates on the ideological level and the pseudo-"socialist market economy" practiced on the implementation level – also referred to as a controlled capitalist economy – that we see. It is true that youth nowadays are neither captivated by the propagandist slogans of the Party discourse, for example Xi Jinping's "China Dream," nor do they practice communism in daily life. But open confrontation with the Party and questioning the legitimacy of the system is also rare – at least hardly anybody in our interviews and ethnographic studies expressed such views. While in the "Western" imagination youth may be perceived to be critical, oppositional, if not rebellious toward domination, Chinese youth, even when they themselves feel subordinated, do not completely refute the value of the Communist Party in China. Still, as a longitudinal study shows, while the number of student Party members increases, they:

> don't show a strong commitment to or even enthusiasm for the Party's orthodox ideology despite the Party's unrelenting ideological and political work on campus. Survey results have repeatedly suggested that they are more concerned about their future job searches or career advancement than realizing communism or building socialism. (Gang 2005: 393)

Chinese youth seem to be primarily pragmatic in opting for being or not being involved in the Party, "although they are unlikely to become advocates of liberal democracy, gradual deviation from orthodox communist ideology will gain momentum" (Gang 2005: 393).

In sum, youth share an ambivalent attitude toward the Party. Partyism limits their possibility of being critical about the Party – thus blocking the option to develop an oppositional ideology. The Party expediently sanctions and censors any outspoken critical public statements on blogs and websites. On the other hand, partyism evolves into a kind of cultural capital – with the footnote that we do understand the meaning it takes in the Chinese context is different from Bourdieu's cultural capital on a social level – that privileges and makes youth feel or act superior in many social relationships. Naturally in a competitive society, many youth, and certainly their parents, weighing the ideological concession or compromise against the real-world advantage, would favor the latter and support Party membership, if only for the sake of securing a job in the near future.

Here we differ from analyses that claim Chinese youth to be lacking in pragmatism. For example, Liang (2012: 185) suggests that Chinese youth are too romantic for their spiritual pursuit, lacking in the pragmatism that the last generation had to embrace in times of revolution. In his view, before China's economic boom that took full swing after 2001, youth were likely to stand firm with their ideals but it appears that youth nowadays go for another extreme. The best example commonly mentioned is an anecdote by university teachers that fewer good students are willing to continue for further studies; directly joining the workforce and occupying a position seems the priority for youth in this fast-changing China. In sum, at a crossroads for job searching and career decision, Chinese youth weigh all the pros and cons about job options, and they make use of their family *guanxi* and contentedly claim their Party membership on job application forms. Being a Party member has evolved in the eyes of youth from an ideological choice toward a choice meant to further one's career and life choices. The Party is not only a network of control, but also a network of both positive and negative influence. Youth have to navigate through this, while holding on to their own values, attitudes, and worldviews.

FAMILY AND FAMILISM

Family, health, and friendship are listed by both the 1980s and the 1990s generation as the three most important things in life (Zou 2011: 72). When 812 Fujian youth were asked for their most important goal in life, 57.4 percent aimed to have a happy family, 52.3 percent wanted a successful career, and 44.2 percent chose good health (Lin 2008: 85). On the question among youth born in the 1990s how they plan to deal with their parents in the future, 63.8 percent want to live with them, 9.9 percent think of hiring a nurse, 7.4 percent think they can take care of themselves, and 3.7 percent want to send them to an old people's home (Yiguanzhiku and Tengxun 2014: 48). The same study also quotes Wei, a 20-year-old kindergarten teacher in Beijing, saying:

> I am very dependent on my parents. I feel that our generation generally
> have a very good relationship with our parents. Maybe because I am
> the only child of my family, my parents give me all their love. I com-
> municate a lot with my parents from childhood on, so I rely on them
> very much. When they get older, they must live together with me.
> (Yiguanzhiku and Tengxun 2014: 37)

As this quote and these figures suggest, there is no doubt that deeply
infiltrating into youth's value system is its own family. If family is a
neutral term, the norm of subscribing to a family or familism itself is
an ideology. By ideology, we mean that the doctrines of a patriarchal
family continue to function as the centripetal force stopping youth
from deviating from social norms, parents' aspiration, and lineage
expectation. Although the extended families of Chinese have over time
changed into numerous nuclear families due to state policy, with major
cities like Beijing and Shanghai reducing to an average of 2.67 persons
per household (in 2007) (HKLSA n.d.: 7), the power of families has
never declined. The power refers not only to the attraction of the
family, but also to the practices, rituals, and norms of family life that
are still very much respected among educated urban youth. During
major festivals and long holidays, for example the Spring Festival and
the long holiday around Labour Day, we have witnessed that young
teenagers studying in Hong Kong skipped their lessons to fly back
home and stay for a short period of time. Within China, like other
migrant workers, "migrant" students also dash back to their home by
all means of transportation.

The question is why youth with an urbanized outlook and cosmopolitan view would adhere to this traditional Confucian legacy, and in
particular renew the patriarchal power with which they are shackled.
When university students are asked why they do not question familial
norms related to marriage, most students would think that this is a
taken-for-granted answer: parental bonding is the strongest among all

social institutions given that the power of the extended Chinese family and influence of religion have waned since the Cultural Revolution. After the disappearance of social institutions (other than Party and formal institutions), society leaves the nuclear family as just about the only private domain (other than a person's individual domain). One could also explicate it in terms of the one child policy since the 1970s. Instead of regarding the policy as creating a structural population problem, we could apprehend youth's psychological dependency on the family given that family life revolves around them. From the parents' viewpoint, their son or daughter is the one in whom they invest all their hope for the future; this increases not only the burden but also results in another sort of close surveillance. There are other problems of course. For example, the loneliness of the only child growing up can also cause psychological problems for youth, which then may lead to violent behavior according to some clinical psychologists in China (Wang 2006).

But we are quite hesitant about accepting such arguments that can suggest moral panics surrounding youth, and that also tend to ideologically subscribe to the norm of the nuclear family with at least two children, thus leaving out other possible forms of family life, such as single or gay parenthood. Our concern is more the formation of youth culture with these youngsters with alleged "psychological deficiencies." Precisely because of the latter, youth are compelled to communicate with other youth outside the family domain, to seek psychological and other immaterial support, as well as simply pleasure. Of particular interest here are online communities in China's social media such as *Weibo* (the Chinese equivalent of Twitter) and *Weixin* (Wechat, the Chinese equivalent of WhatsApp) as we will also show in the coming chapters. In these domains, the function left for the family is deemed to be different. To qualify the new function of the family owing to the reduced family size (Wang 2006), we further highlight that the weight of family moves toward, first, the role of "edification" and, second, the provision of real material and immaterial support, whereas the role of parents as good emotional listeners to youth is starkly reduced, in particular when children move out of the family home and live in cities.

First, family edification here involves passing on, if not imposing, parents' values on their child or, less often, children. It is difficult to illustrate all the diverse ways of value imposition in the family. It ranges from youth's voluntary and docile compliance to familism to the more rocky way of enforcement by incentive and sanction. A more vivid representation of the suppression can be seen in the classic TV drama *Chinese Family: The New Desire* (2009) first broadcast on Shanghai TV Drama channel in 2010. It was a direct reflection of how a family suppresses youth, in which the young couple's childbirth, marriage, and love are highly swayed by the grandmother's bias and traditional values. The TV drama starts with a "row" at a reunion dinner during the Spring Festival. The conflict is about the single child and male sibling of the family Yan who has fallen in love with and married a kindergarten teacher from a mediocre family. When they are pushed toward the verge of divorce, Yan's wife is found to be pregnant which creates a dilemma for their family: a choice between having a grandchild versus defending the wealthy status of the family. The show illustrates that familism is still potent not just on the level of the nuclear family but also across generations.

The strong familism in China is closely related to one of the themes of this book, homosexuality and sexuality, issues that are very much contained, disguised, or made invisible in the family, as we will show in chapter 4. For the discourse of homosexuality, family can be regarded as an earlier filter for managing and controlling values of youth before school and work. For expression of sexuality, family seems to function to delay the proliferation of a sexual discourse, and the discourse might be continuously silenced until marriage or when youth start dating. Although premarital sex among youth is quite common and youth have a favorable attitude toward it, studies in Shanghai show that males simply do not communicate with parents about sex, with only a small portion of female respondents talking to their mother about it (Wang et al. 2007). We thus witness the eradication of any sexual discourse inside the family, also in modern Chinese cities. Here we would like to add that, in line with Foucault, we do not make a normative claim here; the desire or demand to speak about sexuality can also have profound disciplinary implications.

Second, the small nuclear family structure leaves the single child as the family's only descendant. This is not just a kind of familial obligation given to the child. Although having moved to work and study in a big city, they are still affectively entangled with their family, being the only bloodline of the family, and materially implicated as the inheritor of the family properties. In the post-Cultural Revolution era, the sharp social changes and urbanization have not deeply eroded the parent–child relationship; it is assumed, like elsewhere in the world, that parents bequeath their wealth to their only child, and 50–70 percent of the total household income is said to go to the single child (Liu 2013: 58). Before the inheritance, material support to urban youth from their family is common. For the new rich it is not uncommon for parents to purchase a flat for a few million RMB for their child upon marriage. Thus, when one of the major difficulties in life for Chinese urban youth is their solitary life in big cities, family, despite being far away, becomes also a strong source of support. These roles can reverse, however, when the child is older, and the parents are retired. Then it is the children who are financially supportive of their family. Our interview in Hangzhou with a university graduate aged 24, who originally comes from Guangdong province, describes why she ended up working as a young illustrator far away from home:

> I want to stay away from home for study. I thought of going abroad to Hong Kong to study but I really don't want to be too far away from

home. So, I went to Zhuhai (still in Guangdong Province) for study. It is away from home. After graduation, I didn't want to go back home so I came here to do what I wanted to do…My mom is very supportive. So far I can meet my expenses though…I don't want her to know that I'm kind of like that [leading a very meager life in Hangzhou] here.

This young comic illustrator is typical of many Chinese youth; they leave home for university education, end up working in big cities, and communicate with home using social media mostly. Perhaps they never plan to return home and to live again in their hometown, but our interviews with them all confirm that their linkage to the family is still irreplaceable. Many urban students tell quite similar stories. Asked why they came to study in Guangzhou from Guangxi, a student at Jinan University mentions:

I study here because it is not far away from my home [but I'm also leaving home]. I may not go back home to work but I don't want to be too far away from home. My family still worries about me.

At this point, the youth discourse described here seems not very consistent with our earlier claim that youth always attempt to carve out a cultural space to escape from the system, creating an alternative and sometimes even counter-hegemonic space. However, the aim of youth is never to completely desegregate from the cultural control of the family. Chinese youth, while navigating the forces of urbanism, consumerism, and cosmopolitanism, do not necessarily cut off the fetters of "control." These controls, if not too repressive, become a source of material support as well as cultural capital that occasionally accelerates their pace of adaptation in school and work. Among all controls, family is the most resourceful arena for youth.

We would like to stress here that this role of the family is quite persistent. We came across similar narratives among youth in earlier research in 1992 and 1997. In 1997, for example, Zhi Yong told Jeroen de Kloet (in de Kloet 2010: 143–4):

> When I have friction with my parents, I tell myself that they are my parents, that they support me, love me. It's irresponsible of me to make them angry. Of course, it's not always my fault, but I don't think I should make them angry. They work so hard and have experienced so many hardships, I don't want them to feel uneasy.

The empirical question then becomes whether youth feel that family controls too much of their everyday life. Our interviews with youth corroborate our thesis that they do not feel oppressed even though family still has a strong say over their life, including marriage. Among the cases we encountered, matchmaking is still common but it has changed its face: now parents help arrange meetings for their kids in the cities they now live in, with potential candidates coming from the same hometown. Despite being away from their family, unless they relocated at a very early age, their marriage can be pre-arranged with minimal resistance. On the one hand, their family keeps nagging their kids and will try to intervene at any point by choosing the spouse and the age of marriage, even when they live far away. On the other hand, albeit with reticent response and slight enthusiasm, youth may still accede to the marriage and understand the very fact that they are fulfilling the familial duties and piety in marriage. Of course, this does not mean that this leads to a blissful life forever, as figures show that the divorce rate exceeds 30 percent. What we do observe is that although family impacts the generation with very rigid Chinese values, familism is still not the cultural area of contestation for youth.

In the end, familism effectively becomes a value that tactfully molds gender and marriage norms in Chinese society, legitimizing heterosexual love, indexing practices of marriage and family life, and reinforcing the collective roles of monitoring gender norms and values. While studies from the US (e.g. Watson and Ebrey 1991) show that marrying someone primarily for economic reasons is considered unacceptable and sustaining gender inequality, to the local Chinese youth, they might feel comfortable with the limits inherited by the family among all other things. In her study on children, rights, and modernity in China, Orna Naftali (2014) also shows that the discourse about youth's right as autonomous persons coexists with a strong hold on traditional filiality, which is very much in line with our argument that familism is also an enabling force, despite all the constraining factors. If new cultural spaces are formed out of youth's needs and desires, these spaces exist in conjunction with familism so that both youth space and family space can co-exist without much, if any, friction.

PEDAGOGY AND EDUCATION

Educational institutions in China are the most immediate platforms designed to govern youth. For the sake of national development, they are incubation hubs for the future leaders in different domains of the nation. Particularly in the area of science and technology, the education system plays an indispensable role. However, behind these pragmatic agendas, education also primes the role of indoctrinating youth with the ideological imperative of the Party. Under Deng Xiaoping's modernization strategies and the Open Door policy since the 1980s, the educational policy has largely swung toward the pragmatic end. But even today, learning the Party's position, the leaders' ideology, and Marxist doctrines still remains in the curriculum as a legacy of control. Patriotic education constitutes an important part of the curriculum, which feeds into the discourse of nationalism that currently serves as an important ideological glue to hold the nation together (Callahan 2006). In a sense, while ideological education still exists as part of the formal learning (required in curriculum and informal education), indirect control – not through propaganda content in books and examinations – becomes more imminent, as well as more invisible, attesting to the mutations and intensification of (bio-)power in China.

Few studies have studied the forms and formats of education as an indirect social control. Most academic studies on the education system in China focus on its policy reform of the system after the Cultural Revolution and in the 1980s (Price 1970; Bauer et al. 1992; Tsang 1996). These studies mainly help answer the question whether educational reforms could enhance mobilization of the population, reduce class and gender inequalities, and increase efficiencies in terms of uses of government resources. The education system can be analyzed as producing the new generation with ranges of cultural practices and modes of subjectivity that are embedded in the national ideology. These practices range from going along with inflexible (and even unreasonable) rules of school discipline, tolerating the lengthy hours of in-school teaching and out-of-school drilling, self-observing, monitoring and reporting others' daily conduct in school and non-school hours, adapting the standardized knowledge, textbooks, assessment and interpretation accorded by teachers, to name a few. Initiated by teachers in school, the supremacy of the pedagogy diffuses from students to parents who work in tandem with teachers to ensure the seamlessness of the mechanism of the pedagogy. More explicitly, the mechanism works on the basis of an interlocking of time and space between school and family: once youth are relocated from family to school during the nine years of free education, the schools are obligated to shoulder the onus to make sure the kids follow the practices – and the Party's mission – until they internalize it and enforce others to follow it. At different levels of schooling, a parallel Party system is set up to work with the school system to govern the school. At university, the Party secretary is on a par with the president in terms of their position in the institution to rule the university.

The power relationship we describe here then is not so much generated by the content of the education. Rather, it is about the standard behaviors and daily-observed routines; the panoptic environment in the school is to ensure youth perform properly, abide by the norms, and live as docile citizens before they join the workforce in society. Then the entire education and examination system, together with family, not only functions to make children toe the Party line but aims to turn youth into docile citizens. Of course, there are practical concerns. The basic knowledge transfer has to be fulfilled so as to meet the needs of the expanding economy of China. To perpetuate the social norms, pedagogy is also regarded as a part of the value education to bring up children and transform them into talents who could support the aging population in future China, although so far the pragmatic effectiveness of value education is still unproven (Postiglione 2011). That is, no one really knows if the newer generation is really able or willing to support financially their parents when their parents grow old.

Again, the power of education is not something new, it was also there in previous decades, and also then, it caused stress and dismay among Chinese youth. De Kloet quotes Liu Jiayue from an interview in 1997 (2010: 145):

> The education system restricts personalities, and only cares about examinations. I felt that my life in middle school was like life in hell, nothing funny, only those examinations. I think the education system is too cruel, it ruins personalities.

The pressure of the education system in China is exceptionally high (Zhao 2009). In the earlier mentioned study among college students, an overview is given of the main sources of their mental pressure. "Study" ranks highest with 52.1 percent, followed by "employment" (28.2 percent) and "inter-personal relationships" (10 percent) (Shi 2013: 232). Within the education system, if we were asked what the largest social force that "controls" youth nowadays in China is, without hesitation we would say that, of all social institutions, the *gaokao* exam-ination is the most controlling factor. *Gaokao* is the short form of National Higher Education Entrance Examination. It is almost the only conduit for youth to reach higher education institutions immedi-ately after secondary or high school education in China. The year 2006 marked the peak for the numbers of students sitting the examination with 9.5 million youth tackling *gaokao*. Although the number of can-didates sitting the examination is decreasing because of the one child policy, the importance of the examination in the eyes of the rising middle-class family has been ever increasing. "Given its critical impor-tance, the *gaokao* affects every aspect of China's education system. Although it takes place only at the end of high school, its effects trickle down all the way to elementary school and even preschool" (Zhao 2009: 80). The *gaokao* is so demanding that it also steers youth away from thinking creatively or independently, thus leaving hardly any or no space for youth to think alternatively from the state agenda. It is then no surprise that the ultimate goal of primary and secondary school education consists of being successful in the *gaokao*.

The primal allegiance to *gaokao* thus allows the education system to be transformed into a single system, for which we would like to use the term "cage of schooling." China's primary and high school systems operate like cages that imprison youth. An increasing trend in China's major cities, and common in famous elite schools, is toward a system of boarding schools. The formalization of the boarding school echoes very much the official and common discourse of gender and work in Chinese society. Under the constitution of the PRC, females were expected to make up an equal part of the workforce following a gender equality discourse. According to Mao, women hold up half of the sky. Under a more modern urban discourse, with a nucleus family as its epicenter, both the wife and the husband are part of the workforce to meet the high cost of living in a city, resulting in the need for the children to be "babysat" in schools. Parents largely support such whole-life schooling as they believe this will push up their children's academic scores and that eventually they could outperform others in the *gaokao* and obtain a green card to university. Even without choosing to study in boarding schools, many parents in cities are very willing to pay high fees for their children to stay after school for extra classes or go to cram schools to prepare for examinations. Of course, eventually, the higher education system is preparing children for entrepreneurship to drive the economy of the state (Turner and Acker 2002; Zhao 2009).

As one could imagine, keeping youth almost full time in fixed locales from primary to lower and upper secondary schools becomes a *de facto* blockage of external ideologies, global values, and deviant ideas from the Internet, that may challenge and refute the status quo and the education system. Given that it is hard for alternative cultures to infiltrate into this educational system, what is taught, rehearsed, and propagandized in schools becomes the only version of truth and knowledge, one that is catering to the effective ruling of the state. Because youth are trapped in the schools, first, religious thoughts and other external influences are completely shut off. Second, youth at this stage of schooling are also separated from global culture in which different gender values and consumption values may be articulated, although they may be more exposed to global culture online at their university stage, as we will illustrate in the coming chapters. Although regulations limit the use of Internet in schools, the penetration of the Internet remains the highest in China for people aged between 10 and 29 (CNNIC 2015). Given the control over other media, the Internet is probably the widest channel of alternative opinions in high school and, especially, university.

On the one hand, the centralized education system, from knowledge to daily routines, is now being used as an effective tool to routinize, regulate and train youth behavior, rules, norms, and thoughts. It is this process of governmentality and related modes of subjectivation that help us understand how power and authority become internalized. To maintain the system intact, educators' surveillance and supervision over youth is also annexed to the pedagogy patrolling over youth to ensure full compliance. As youth feel accustomed to the system, the surveillance evolves into a disciplinary gaze with the effect that youth develop the feeling of being constantly observed by teachers even when they are not being watched. But the power is not only panoptic, the biopower penetrates deeply into the senses and indeed technologies of the young self, the school offers modes of subjectivity that promise a bright future, and these desired selves support the current status quo.

Also, due to spatial arrangements and control of student movements, fluidity of student flow is reduced to a minimum. Many primary schools and middle schools are joined so that students living in a certain neighborhood and community will follow steadily and stay long enough in the pipeline of control. Only a few assessments after the middle schools and the *gaokao* are mechanisms to relocate youth to other educational institutions. Existing students can hardly escape out of the pipeline, nor can someone from without easily squeeze into the system. The state would dissuade outsiders, namely foreign students or returning Chinese students holding a foreign passport without local *hukou*, from entering this system to avoid that the former might pervert the "purified" youth in the system. Unless the students hold foreign passports and are willing to pay exorbitant tuition fees for international schools, youth with the registered household accounts or *hukou* have to remain within certain designated institutions in the city. In our study in Beijing, we managed to talk to a Hong Kong couple working for a mobile phone company in Beijing, who sent their children to an international school near the neighborhood where they live. Basically the parents have no alternative because their children are not eligible to study in the local educational system; these children could only choose the educational alternatives such as international schools in China.

In the end, there is a hegemonic pedagogy system tacitly agreed upon among educators, parents, and youth. Practicing the same rationality, endorsing the standardized schooling and achieving flying colors in examinations become a united goal among all parties concerned. The consequence is that schooling, except the part of knowledge transfer, is equivalent to a social training program for 12 years from primary to high school. For both parents and children, they are obliged to feel guilty and anxious when they deviate from the disciplinary norm and conduct (Foucault 1980). Self-regulation and self-discipline in the system doubly freeze any possible changes within schooling.

In a nutshell, the control of the life world of youth can be encapsulated in the concepts of time and space (Giddens 1982). Time and space are constituent elements of all social actions and interactions (Gross 1982: 83), and by means of limiting the time and space where interactions take place, youth's capacities, formation of values, and mobilization power are all contained within the state's limit. Schooling, the modes of pedagogy and the demanding test-based examination system, basically command youth's use and definition of space and time. If the limits are exceeded or the boundaries set by the conduct agreed upon by themselves are crossed, youth will face immediate sanctions. The latter includes physical punishment by teachers, being turned into an outcast by peer groups, stigmatization of being a loser in public examinations, being denied university entry, or being penalized by being given McJobs, to name a few. In the previous domains mentioned, partyism and familism, violation of Party dogma and family order might only result in verbal warning and familial admonishment respectively. However, in the education system, failure to fully comply with the disciplines that underlie the pedagogy will have concrete consequences: no future, no career, or permanently being forced out of the urban setting.

CONCLUSION

In this chapter, our major aim of elucidating these three emblematical macro cultural controls is to map the regimes Chinese youth cultures have to negotiate. In a time of intense globalization, we may expect that with more resources available to youth today – both material and non-material – they are better equipped to contest the political control of the state, explore different cultural scripts beyond the demands of the school, family, and state, and to imagine a whole new world. Nevertheless, the story that we want to tell is not this Disneyesque perfect happy ending story. In the "skillfully constructed" youth environment in China, the assumption of a youth being liberalized by global culture is highly questionable. Although it might not be entirely wrong, youth's own growth, reasoning, and conduct are not completely free. What we can label as the "cultural firewall of China," one that is built alongside the Great Firewall of China that serves as the proxy of the Internet that filters something from outside, helps to fence off influences from other cultures. In reality, the cultural firewall is a quite effective device that delays and dilutes the influence of the Internet. Many studies (e.g. Liu 2013) arguably suggest that the Internet in China could potentially inflict changes on youth values and life. While we agree to a certain extent, we also want to suggest that, especially during the long stage of early adolescence, the cultural firewall curtails the power of external influence, and only a limited amount of potentially counter-hegemonic values can potentially reach Chinese youth. Counter-hegemonic resources are more easily reachable by youth for those aged 18 or above – a period when they start to go to university. But by then, the cultural firewall has already folded youth into the discourses that sustain the state, the family, and the school.

What are the chances that this cultural firewall will be demolished? These chances seem slim. This may sound like a very pessimistic future for the next generation of China. But our observation is that, after acknowledging this partly self-constructed cultural firewall, this does not mean that all Chinese youth are turned into docile citizens or a homogeneous horde. Youngsters also work collectively with their peers, to elicit creative expression and self-improvement, to survive and occasionally even destabilize the system (Kipnis 2012). These technologies of the self, or youth's subjectivities that may mutate from the desired subjectivities as promoted by state, school, and family, are the ones that hold the potential to deviate and disrupt.

The occasional connection and disconnection of youth from the state, school, and family thus make youth's behavior sometimes unpredictable, uncontrollable, and academically intriguing. Such (dis)connection can be magnified or dimmed by various factors as we will see in the other chapters in this book. China's own "Youth Cultural Phenomenon Report" – released in 2004 – which primarily aimed to gauge the impact of popular culture on youth and develop solutions for the state, mentioned that "cultural groupings" have become one of the major forces that shake the structure of society. These cultural categories, besides being classified by various factors such as socio-economic background, class, family attributes, now assume new forms clustered by blogging, mobility, and petite bourgeoisie (*xiaozi*), to name a few (Yang and Zhang 2005). While we recognize that almost all grown-up youth are netizens nowadays (Clark 2012), we want to steer away from a simple technological determinism that reads the Internet as a liberating force. Also, even though youth are exposed to global culture, values of democracy, and liberalism, the lingering influence of family, education, and the Party serves as a powerful antidote – as we have argued in this chapter.

In China, academics like to use the term *cabianqiu* to describe intellectuals or dissident attempts to use the grey area of politics to challenge domination. Cultural workers such as television producers also use the term to rationalize their production that legally is allowed and yet it touches the very political baseline allowed by the authorities. But in youth's terrain, the relationship between hegemony and counter-hegemony is more complex; it is not always an oppositional relationship. For all the state-planned or represented institutions, Party, family, and schools, they sometimes animate youth's own development, extend their resources, prime their capacity, and provide both emotional and material support for youth. Youth, in particular vulnerable youth in urban settings, need them and sometimes hold on to these domains and institutions.

This illustrates how power intensifies and seeps through every detail of everyday life. If youth are not in line with it, they do not challenge the system by testing the baseline of the institutions through *cabianqiu*. They are displaying an alternative version of the institutions in terms of expression, representation, and cultural practices. Examples commonly found are graffiti art in the urban setting, *shanzhai* or parodic and mocking imitations of CCTV shows, political satire using the nicknames of political leaders found on *Weibo*, to name a few. Thus, this book focuses less on the uncompromising or radical youth who aim to revolutionize politics and the conscious youngsters who are dedicated to changing social norms in contemporary China, although both will also feature in our analyses. But "youth culture" in this book is more about the larger and less outspoken cohort of youngsters who are busy producing, distributing, negotiating, switching back and forth, locating and dislocating the dominant culture in specific cultural realms, occasionally acquiring cultural resources, and creating a new sense of space at certain historical points of time. The dislocation of the dominant culture can be understood as displacing it with some "alternative" culture with a possible and sporadic and subtle impact on the former.

The state is now quite aware of the cultural practices of "slightly" divergent youth, which the authorities and academics would not label as "youth problems" as they would have done a decade ago. These include the widely reported lesbian marriage, though without legal status, on Tencent news; the collective cheating in the *gaokao* examination; and, more often on entertainment news, the thousands of "obsessed" fans waiting for their idols at the airport. In spite of such controversies, the official views offered are nowadays quite diverse, incongruent and non-definitive. In the previous chapter we presented figures that allude to increased skepticism of Chinese youth toward the authorities, while in this chapter other studies show their commitment to values related to China's rejuvenation and socialism with Chinese characteristics. One study explains youth's emerging culture as alienated culture in a Chinese Marxist vocabulary (Ren 2003). The study identified various kinds of cultural alienation (e.g. idol worship, youth clothing, and uses of accessories) in the domains of language, symbols, values, norms, and behavioral patterns. The very meaning of alienation is that there are new cultural spaces from the official point of view, dislocated from mainstream culture. Alternative as they are, the new spaces might not yet severely undermine the Party, family, and schooling, all of which are by and large still left intact. Social and political behavior in China is closely related to the art of the possible; Chinese youth take a pragmatic approach, even when they demand less hierarchy or more democracy, they will and can only articulate that to a limited extent in public (Shi 2015). This mode of "feigned compliance" could eventually crumble, if the conditions of possibility change: that what now seems solid may indeed evaporate. But for the time being, we do not see signs this will indeed be the case.

Thus, the state's response to such irregularity or "cultural alienation" is mild and ad hoc. In a study of idolatry and youth fans, Yue (2007: 37–8) documented different levels of media response toward the hype of fans' behavior toward the contestants in the *Super Girl* phenomenon from 2004 to 2006 in China, which we analyze in chapter 3, finding a wide range of discourse spanning from conservative comments suggesting it perverts youth to the view that one should "respect the public's reasonable demand" while claiming at the same time that we should accentuate social responsibility among "the wide range of choices." In other words, the state tends to become more tolerant toward the cultural practices of today's youth.

How, then, do youth navigate through these multiple forces of state, school, and family; how do they find their own space, their own dreams, their own possibilities? Since we started our research in the early 1990s, as we have alluded to in this chapter as well, we have witnessed similar questions, producing like-minded struggles over identity. But such struggles are not played out in the same way. The power of the institutions analyzed in this chapter proves quite resilient. But the opportunities to develop cultural tactics as a way to negotiate this power, tactics that are simultaneously implicated in the intensification of power – after all, there is no outside to the system – seem to have multiplied. The disjuncture between the ideoscape of the state, school, and family and the mediascape of China, produces opportunities for youth to produce *moments* in which they carve out their own space. That can happen during a rock festival, when they are collectively hypnotized by the sound and words of Zuoxiao Zuzhou, it can be when they vote for their favorite music star, when they write poems about their suffering and publish these online, or when they discuss the differences between the original reality show *Running Man* and its Chinese translation, differences that alert them to issues deemed sensitive by the censors. In the remaining chapters of this book, we hope to uncover such examples, and show how also there, power seeps through, infiltrates and penetrates into everyday life, both enabling as well as disabling certain subject positions. In the end, to come back to Liang Qichao with whose words we opened this chapter, we are not quite convinced that youth are moving forward, rather, their movements strike us as rhizomic, fragmented, and dispersed.

2

Dressing Up the Future: Chinese Youth Today

We don't want to copy you
We don't want to become you
We don't want to follow you
We don't want to change into you
New Pants (in *Follow Follow*, 2011)

INTRODUCTION

In the 2011 movie *Follow Follow* (*Yuedui*), directed by rock singer Peng Lei, a ghost appears in Beijing, arriving on a flying saucer. It is a white man with shoulder-length blond hair. When he turns around, we see Nirvana's lead-vocalist Kurt Cobain. Indeed, Cobain returns to life in 2011, this time in a bedroom in Beijing. Since his suicide in 1994, he has been a cult figure in the Chinese underground scene, signifying the ultimate rock-and-roll hero. At the end of the movie, however, Cobain confesses that rock does not belong to China. "Why do Chinese people like rock-and-roll music?" he wonders, "I think it is just curiosity, later they get bored with it." Then he claims, "So many people were calling me in China, I had to come to China. I don't belong here. I have to go."

The specter of Western popular culture is literally haunting China in this movie. Somehow, Cobain is quite wrong in his assertion: Chinese rock music has been around now since the mid-1980s, and is not likely to disappear. Furthermore, as the work of Paul Clark (2012) convincingly argues, the music is not to be read solely as Western either, in its lyrics and its spirit, we can also trace alliances between the songs and sounds of the Red Guards and those of rock music. Indeed, Chinese rock singers and bands have also appropriated communist styles in their imagery (Mao caps, red scarves) and songs (appropriations of communist classics). But, as Jeroen de Kloet has argued elsewhere, Chinese rock musicians do face a problem of authenticity:

> Rock is driven by a quest for authenticity. For Chinese, this authenticity operates as a deadlock: if a Chinese rock singer like Zuoxiao Zuzhou mimics a global rock aesthetics, he will be blamed by journalists in and outside China for being a copycat. Were he to add Chinese elements to his sound, such as *pipa* or *guzheng*, he would be accused of exoticism or self-orientalism. Zuoxiao Zuzhou is thus stalked by a double-edged sword of authenticity. (2014: 7)

Creativities and youth subcultural styles that emerge outside the "West" constantly carry the burden of geopolitical representation as authenticating proof. Whereas "the West" can claim to make universal rock music, in China, this has to be *Chinese* rock music (de Kloet 2010).

Peng Lei's articulation of China being out of sync with rock culture in the movie *Follow Follow* in the end paradoxically authenticates his position: it is a claim of inauthenticity, a claim of incompatibility that turns him both authentic and compatible with global rock culture. It is through embracing both edges of the sword of authenticity simultaneously that he manages to negotiate his authenticity. In the theme song of the movie, "I don't want to imitate you" (*wo bu xiang mofang ni*), the New Pants, of which director Peng Lei is the lead vocalist, sing that they are not the Ramones or Joy Division, they are not artists, they don't listen to pop music, go to the Internet, or do karaoke. Peng assures the listener that they "don't want to copy you," indeed, they don't want to follow you, change into you, or become you.

But, we all know that they go on the Internet, that they are artists. The clip itself is set in New York, rather than China. "I don't want to imitate you" is performed in the center of that "you": New York. This playful and ironic denial of the other, be it the West, pop, or karaoke culture, constitutes at the same time an affirmation and embracing of that other. In their clearly exaggerated juxtaposition of binaries, the New Pants move beyond the geopolitical deadlock of global authenticity – they don't want to become you, because they already are you (example taken from de Kloet 2014).

The movie presents a love story and is set in contemporary Beijing. Like their Western counterparts, youth is drifting, alienated from society, spending time in bars, trying to find funky fashion items in small shops tucked away in the little alleys of Beijing, they are loitering around, and trying to become a rock star. When we bring back to mind the masses of Red Guards in their identical Mao suits with similar hairstyles, the current display of different youth styles indeed offers a striking contrast. This chapter aims to delve into these emerging youth cultural styles. After further elaborating on the links between youth styles and globalization, we will explore emerging fashion styles in China, its music cultures, and, finally, its online manifestations.

GLOBAL INAUTHENTICITIES

In an insightful overview of globalization theories, Diana Crane (2002) distinguishes four different models of cultural globalization (see table 2.1). The first, cultural imperialism, argues that the global economic and cultural system is dominated by the advanced countries that dominate third world cultures. This model remains quite dominant in journalistic discourses on globalization, and predicts an increased homogenization of culture. The second model emerged as a response; it argues that the world is becoming more complex and more heterogeneous. Rather than dividing the world into a center and periphery,

Table 2.1. Models of cultural globalization

MODEL	PROCESS OF CULTURAL TRANSMISSION	PRINCIPAL ACTORS, SITES	POSSIBLE CONSEQUENCES
Cultural imperialism Media imperialism	Center–periphery	Global media conglomerates	Homogenization of culture
Cultural flows/ networks	Two-way flows	Regional and national conglomerates and corporations	Hybridization of culture
Reception theory	Center–periphery; multidirectional	Audiences, publics, entrepreneurs, gatekeepers	Negotiation, resistance
Cultural policy strategies, e.g. preservation, resistance, reframing, glocalization	Framing of national cultures	Global cities, museums, heritage sites, cultural memory, media, ministries of culture and trade	Competition, negotiation

Source: Crane 2002: 2

this model argues that there are multiple centers, that serve as nodal points for a complex network of global cultural flows that results in an increased hybridization of culture. The third model concerns the reception of culture, and as such operates on a quite different analytic level when compared to the other two models. Here the emphasis lies on the reception of culture, arguing that *even if* the whole world watched James Bond, they will do so with different eyes. The fourth model again operates at a different analytical level, and stresses the importance of cultural policy strategies and institutional arrangements, in particular related to the government. One can think here of quotas set by the Chinese state on the number of Hollywood releases per year, 20 per year prior to 2012, and 34 films a year since then (Rosen 2015), or the creative industry policies that result in the rapid emergence of creative clusters and districts in Chinese cities.

All models remain valid today. When looking at the production of culture, television formats are often sold globally, producing a similar and indeed homogenized logic of media production. Audiences world-wide are watching blockbuster movies and television series. But when a similar format is being sold, its translation for the local or national media culture involves numerous slippages of meaning and different appropriations. In this book, our analyses refer back to each of the four models, but when it comes to explain how globalized culture today is plugged into everyday lifestyles of Chinese youth, we draw primarily on the second model and its conceptualization of cultural globalization as a networked flow of cultures in which different centers of production dominate. In the case of China, apart from the United States, also South Korea, Japan, Taiwan, and Hong Kong are important cultural sources of inspiration and indeed appropriation (Chow and de Kloet 2013). Whereas in this chapter, we delve more into "Western" cultural forms and their appropriation in China, especially rock music, in the following chapter we will engage with these inter-Asian cultural flows (Chua 2004, 2012).

Thus, even when more centers of cultural production proliferate, some centers are more important than others, and flows do not flow automatically. In his seminal piece on globalization, Arjun Appadurai (1996) distinguishes flows of people, money, technologies, media, and ideas, each of which constitute a specific scape (the ethno-scape, technoscape, financescape, mediascape, and ideoscape), as we discussed already in the introduction. Crucial in his view are the disjunctures that emerge between these different scapes, for example, whereas the ideoscape in China remains quite closed, its mediascape has, also due to new technologies, rapidly opened up. Thus, whereas new ideas and lifestyles have entered China through different media, despite (but also because of) the attempts to censor some of them, the ideologies as articulated by the nation-state often seem increasingly out of joint. These frictions and tensions, predicted by Appadurai already at that time, propel a wide array of tensions and disjunctures, including the rise of different forms of nationalism.

Finally, debates around cultural globalization are often connected to the thorny issue of authenticity. As we already explained in the introduction to this chapter, in places outside the West, the issue of authenticity often becomes entangled with the burden of geopolitical representation. How to guarantee one's authenticity as a Chinese rock musician, given that he or she operates in a field that is driven by the ideology of authenticity? Elsewhere, de Kloet (2010) shows how different tactics of Sinification help to authenticate Chinese rock. At the same time, as also the example of the movie *Follow Follow* shows, over the past decade, parallel to the rise of China, the burden of Chinese-ness, or to make rock with Chinese characteristics, seems to have weakened significantly. The new generation is less concerned with making rock that sounds or looks Chinese. We can trace a similar distancing from the issue of Chineseness in other cultural fields, like contemporary art and cinema. This, of course, does not mean that the issue has disappeared, the global gaze on Chinese cultural productions continues to demand Chineseness. The latter demand, indeed, will make the chances of Chinese rock becoming global less strong, since Western audiences and journalists often still expect something different and exotic from China. It thus comes as no surprise that one band that tours regularly globally is Hanggai, a band that is dressed up in traditional Chinese costume and that combines "Chinese" sounds with "Western" rock. The double-edged sword of authenticity – if you "just" make rock music you run the danger of being accused of being a mere copycat, whereas if you include strong Chinese elements, you may be accused of self-orientalization and exoticism – keeps on haunting cultural production, and youth culture, in China.

Rather than getting stuck in the issue of authenticity, it makes more sense to see the world as a warehouse of cultural scenarios or scripts that due to media technologies have become available for most people nowadays. When Beijing punk band Brain Failure express their discontent with disco culture in the song "Funky Disco," they not only appropriate the global style of punk, with Mohawks, a screaming voice, and signs of rebellion and anarchism, they also refer back to a punk–disco debate that raged especially in the UK in the late 1970s, but that has never been part of the Chinese cultural landscape. Appadurai refers to this as a "nostalgia without memory.... The past is now not a land to return to in a simple politics of memory. It has become a synchronic warehouse of cultural scenarios" (Appadurai 1996: 30). The continuous revival of cultural forms, be they from the 1960s, 1970s, 1980s, or more recent decades, attests to the continuous recycling and reappropriation of culture, and today, this is taking place on a global scale. The question whether and how authentic these cultural forms are has become obsolete; instead, the question is what these forms enable, what cultural practices they make possible with which social, political, and economic implications. The question of originality, of cultural purity, is turning into a question of cultural practice and cultural dialogue and appropriation. After all, in the words of Michael Taussig, "[T]here is no 'context' anymore, other than cascading glimpses of splintered Othernesses on the world screen of mechanically reproduced imagery. In this world the glimpse, like the sound-bite and the after-image, is where the action is, Dada-like impulsions of Othernesses hurled at disconcerted beings splayed open to the future" (1993: 249).

FASHION STYLES

The connection between fashion, style, and identity has been explored extensively in different studies (Barnard 2007; Entwistle 2000, 2009; Kaiser 2013; Steele 2010). When looking at the global fashion world, China is conspicuously absent. Antonia Finnane (2005: 65) mentions that Pierre Cardin stated in 2002 that Chinese fashion would be sure to become very strong, and that "China will become one of the leading countries for couture." However, this still seems a long road to walk. As Finnane writes, "Western reports on fashion in China routinely sound a note of surprise and discovery, as though Chinese people were still to be seen wearing Mao suits" (2005: 65). But when we walk along the alleys in Shanghai we witness numerous fashion boutiques, often with items made by local designers, catering for the young and hip Chinese. In the streets we see a dazzling variety of styles, most of which allude to a global style with jeans, down jackets and the like – more often than not coming from either H&M or Uniqlo. The cultural imperialism thesis as discussed earlier seems apt to describe the styles we encounter in the streets of Chinese cities. But this would do injustice to the variety in styles, some of which include references to the past, that we come across in the big cities of China.

Till today fashion styles, while being deeply entrenched in a global neoliberal economy, continue to negotiate if not challenge the everyday. In a journal article, Li Changsong warns of the increased vulgarization of Chinese youth, after already critiquing the lack of values and excessive individualization:

> Beauty Fashion, to some degree, gives rise to the phenomenon of vulgarization. And the youth's irrational pursuit of weirdness and

exaggeration breeds their spiritual needs for superficial and vulgar things. All these have hindered the improvement of values, making the values of some young people show the characteristics of vulgarization. (2013: 16)

Such narratives articulate a discourse of "youth as problem" that we analyzed already in the introduction. Such discourses are often mapped onto the domain of fashion. A story of the stocking comes to mind here. Matthew Chew (2003, 2007) discusses in his work two styles that seem quite particular to China: the exposed stocking style that was en vogue in the 1980s and 1990s, and the revival of the *qipao* through the 1990s. Whereas the first case tells us a story of class, style, and globalization, the latter adds an element of cultural nostalgia to the conceptual mix.

To begin with, a confession may be in place here: Jeroen de Kloet's first trip to China was in 1992. He remembers vividly the popularity of exposed short stockings among Chinese women. From his view, this was clearly a sign of bad taste, as Chew writes, according to Western conventions, "women's hosiery should be long enough to have the first several inches of the top of the stocking covered from view by pants or skirt" (2003: 479). It was with these eyes that he observed and judged these styles. What the stockings do – like the pajamas people often wear on the streets in Shanghai – is blur the line between underwear and outerwear, as well as between the public and the private. As Chew describes,

Exposed short stockings transgress the boundary between outerwear and underwear, violating current conventions of decent dressing by displaying a part of dress that is deemed necessary to be kept hidden from public view. The practice represents an act of cultural localization that resists, counteracts, or even neutralizes Western cultural dominance and global homogenization. (2003: 481)

In Chew's reading, deviant styles present an act of resistance, and de Kloet's own bewilderment when watching the stockings smacks of a cultural arrogance that we critiqued earlier already regarding the evaluation of rock music from China. Sadly, in his analysis Chew describes how these hegemonic standards in the end prevail. In Hong Kong the stockings were seen as a sign of bad taste, thus confirming the cultural stereotype that mainland Chinese's sense of fashion is way behind that of Hong Kong. As Chew notes, "the Hong Kong discourse on exposed short stockings was harsh, sarcastic, and contemptuous" (2003: 487). He quotes a middle-aged Hong Kong woman saying "Those short stockings looked so weird. How did they manage to invent such a style? They could not afford long hosiery?" (2003: 487). During the 1980s and 1990s, Hong Kong still served as a role model for mainland China in terms of consumption and lifestyle. Hence, the negative discourse slowly spilled over to the big cities in China, and the exposed stocking fashion style became associated with backwardness and migrants. Now, the stockings have mostly disappeared, and if someone wears them, they will be frowned upon. As such, the boundaries have been redrawn, the border between the outside and the inside, the public and the private, has become stable again. It comes as no surprise that the city of Shanghai banned its citizens from wearing pajamas in public during the Olympic year of 2008; after all, the nation had to be dressed properly under the surveilling eyes of the foreign visitors.

Another example of localization is the return of older Chinese styles in contemporary fashion. At punk concerts, one can come across fans wearing the red scarf and the striped shirts of the Communist Youth League. These have now come to signify rebellion. Shanghai Tang is a label that reinvents Chinese styles, the *qipao* for women and the *changshan* for men, in a contemporary way. The return of the *qipao* is telling for a resurgence of nostalgic nationalism in China. While being marginalized over the past decades, the dress has made a comeback, not so much in everyday street wear as in official occasions and for specific functions, such as waitresses in restaurants. But Chew warns against a reading of the dress solely in terms of a nationalist style; he shows that "the contemporary qipao has received very limited formal and substantive backing" (2007: 147). It has strong connotations with Chineseness, which is not the same as nationalism. For that reason, it has also appeared in the collections of numerous global designers, ranging from Dries van Noten to Miu Miu, an appropriation with clear orientalist implications.

For young people in the big cities, wearing either the *qipao* or the *changshan* will likely be like an ironic dressing up. It resembles the old China, just like the Mao costume connotes the communist China – both tropes are played with, are cheerfully adopted as a localizing tactic, to be swiftly abandoned and be replaced by a Levi's 501. But for others, it will still be a way to be stylish. Chew quotes his informant Monica, who wears very stylish *qipaos* in unexpected combinations with military jackets, boots and silver accessories. She explains:

> Qipao's are [economically] cheap and their effect is good. They are so hard to carry though; I can't wear it that often…It has to be tamed through DIYing or mix-and-matching – I mean, it's unconventional for settings such as this [dance club]. I have to think hard…and pick from as wide a range of stylistic elements and accessories as possible to alter the tone of my qipao. (2007: 155)

The *qipao* is creatively turned into a fashion item by Monica. Chew distinguishes such uses of the dress to express a sense of fashion, be it in Monica's use or as a high fashion item – from uses to express an ethnic or cultural belonging (for example by overseas Chinese students who study in China and connect the dress to their ancestors) and uses to negotiate one's sexiness.

Chew explains how in the second and third tier cities of China, it remains a delicate matter to wear clothes that are too sexy and reveal too much of the body. He quotes Jenny, a 24-year-old office secretary living in Wuhan:

> There are no problems when I stay within the bounds of hip shopping malls, cafes, restaurants and dance clubs. But before I go out, my parents would have a chance to lecture me. When I walk past the neighborhood, people would stare at me.... I definitely hate to run into my co-workers when I'm strolling in the streets in my low-cut jeans and tiny tops. Their gossip at the workplace is not merely annoying, it could cost me my job. (2007: 157)

Social control in public areas thus impacts upon the freedom to wear what one really likes, and this impact will be severely gendered, it is predominantly the female body that needs to be controlled and covered. The *qipao*, in Chew's reading, allows for a renegotiation, its sexiness is coupled to an elegance – as was so clearly demonstrated in Wong-kar Wai's movie *In the Mood for Love*, in which Maggie Cheung showcased 26 *qipao*s – that helps to pacify the normative gaze of the older generation and one's peers. Chew quotes one informant stating that:

> Qipaos may not be as super-trendy as regular [global] fashion and you seldom get a chance to wear them. But they somehow soothe my thirst for fashion. That's why I'm getting into it and other traditional Chinese styles lately.... I'm so tired of getting pestered by my friends and parents because of my [trendy and sexy] clothes. (2007: 158)

Thus, "fashionable, yet not outlandish, sexy yet subdued, *qipao*s represent one of the solutions in China's fashion market that alleviates urban women's fashion dilemma" (Chew 2007: 159–60).

We came across one curious example of how styles continue to re-emerge in 798, the creative art district in Beijing. The district, as a hip quarter, is often used as a site for wedding-picture taking; it reflects a modern lifestyle, a China of the twenty-first century. Normally, the couples themselves are dressed up in normal wedding attire. This time, however, the couple was dressed up in a Cultural Revolution outfit. It is hard to explain or understand such a reappropriation, to read it as a nostalgic act seems out of place, also given the age of the couple, to interpret it a validation or celebration of the Cultural Revolution seems equally problematic. It seems more likely to read it as a performance of difference, an attempt to be original, and as such an identity claim, one that denotes Chineseness and youth, more than communism or rebellion.

The nylon stockings have by and large disappeared from the streets of Chinese cities, the Chinese styles of the *qipao* are omnipresent, but only in specific sectors; what dominates is, like other places in the world, jeans and like-minded "hip" clothing styles. The story of fashion seems to be above all a story of globalization and modernization; in China's subcultures, we witness an experimentation with style that resembles New York and Tokyo, although arguably the latter remains Asia's prime locale for youth fashion. Fashion styles emerge from what Entwistle (2009) calls the tacit aesthetic knowledge of its consumers, a knowledge that is both embodied and expressive, one that marks a sense of distinction, constitutes a display of cultural capital and, for some, also of economic capital (the latter being flaunted by Louis Vuitton bags and the like). This latter observation gestures toward a cultural difference between China and the West: why is it that especially Italian brands like Prada and Dolce & Gabbana and French brands like Louis Vuitton and Dior are so popular among consumers in China? In Asia, more so than in Europe, it seems more possible to display one's economic wealth in public. Hence in art district 798 we can come across an artist driving his Ferrari. Brands like Louis Vuitton or Prada are quite loud in their styles and branding – one can immediately see this is a Louis Vuitton bag (although it remains obscure whether this is a real or a fake one). As such, they constitute clear markers of economic capital, and this translation towards cultural capital is different from what we see in Europe. Bourdieu's work on cultural distinction requires some specific cultural translation when we use it in China (Kuipers 2014).

One last phenomenon that plays an important role in the diffusion of youth fashion styles is the *shanzhai* phenomenon. The term refers to a fortified mountain village outside official control; it stands for the culture of fake products that are produced in primarily Shenzhen. "The term evokes a sense of illegality and subversion: it is copying, but not quite, as there is more to it than just copying" (de Kloet and Scheen 2013: 3; Lin and Fung, 2013). Because of the availability of *shanzhai* fashion items, it is now also possible for people with less money to wear Prada while carrying a Paul Smith bag. While it is risky to read the production of the fake solely in terms of postcolonial resistance towards the hegemony of Western brands, as Ziauddin Sardar (2000) does, it does make luxury brands more available for youth. Neither do we want to follow Ackbar Abbas' teleological contention that "fake production ceases or diminishes when a city or a nation becomes more integrated into the global establishment, at which point strict copyright laws begin to be passed, partly as a result of intellectual property pressure from global companies and states" (Abbas 2008: 254). Whereas China entered the WTO already in 2001, its *shanzhai* culture did not diminish at all. On the contrary, in Shenzhen we can find not only the latest Paul Smith bags and clothes, but also additional items that are inspired by the label but actually designed in China. Just like a *shanzhai* iPhone often has more functions than the original, so do new and unique originals emerge, even when they are fake. As such, the authentic and the fake are mutually constitutive. It has helped to blur the line between high and popular fashion, and allowed Chinese youth to experiment with brands and styles that would remain otherwise out of reach. *Shanzhai* culture is part and parcel of the emergence of fashion styles in China, rather than being counterproductive (see also de Kloet and Scheen 2013; Wong 2013).

China has become more than a market for fashion. Designer Lü Yan from the label Comme Moi explains:

> When it comes to fashion or design people still refer to Paris, Milan, New York and maybe a few other places as the key hubs. China is primarily seen just as a market, where brands want to be and to sell. However, great designers such as Alexander Wang and Phillip Lim are starting to change international perceptions. I also believe that people outside China know now that Chinese brands can produce high-quality designed products. (Williams 2015: 49)

To conclude this section on fashion in China, let us move to Xander Zhou, who has become over the past few years one of China's renowned fashion designers. After being trained in the Netherlands, he has returned to Beijing to start his own studio, and is now one of China's most prolific designers. He distances himself from the burden of geopolitical representation, he explains in an interview: "It's too much, I don't want the burden to glorify my Chineseness through high collars and woven buttons; it's not my job to spread Chinese culture. I am one designer. It's too heavy for me" (Huang 2012). Also, when we look at his website xanderzhou.com (accessed January 26, 2015), we can observe a quite clear distancing from the burden of geopolitical representation. There, he states:

> Preserving traditional culture through fashion might be respectful towards tradition, but it is not respectful towards fashion. I think it is wrong to suppose that anything coming from China should per definition be distinctly Chinese. Some people think that only clothes that have dragons or peonies on them are "really Chinese."

Consequently, there are no or hardly any references to Chineseness in his style; instead, his creations are avant-garde, they bring to mind the subtle qualities of Japanese fashion design, and when presented on a catwalk in Paris we may wonder if people would know this is a Chinese fashion designer. But, as we explained earlier, he remains trapped in that box, and it will be difficult to fully escape, as even a refusal to include specific cultural signifiers can and will still be read as an articulation of one's cultural identity. Other designers opt for the localizing move. For example, Mao Jihong and Ma Ke from the label Exception claim, as a kind of fashionable blending of Xi Jinping's "China Dream" with global capitalism:

> Exception is a representative Chinese clothing brand and the lifestyle and philosophy it advocates reflect the spirit of contemporary China. Exception will provide European and American customers with Chinese-style lifestyle products, while also promoting the Chinese way of life. (in Williams 2015: 73)

Xander Zhou has also been a prominent media figure, and he openly acknowledges his gay identity. The cover of the Gay China issue of the *iLook* magazine that was released in 2009 is striking in this respect. On the cover, we see Xander Zhou in a flamboyant outfit, with big Chinese characters 中国真高兴 (*zhongguo zhen gaoxing*), meaning China is very happy. This is a tongue-in-cheek reference to the nationalist bestseller 中国不高兴 (*zhongguo bu gaoxing*), *Unhappy China*, by Song Xiao Jun (2008). Through this queering of Chinese nationalism, Xander Zhou aligns fashion with politics in a playful way.

SONIC STYLES

A lot has changed over the past two decades when we look at music cultures in China. In his book on youth culture in China, Paul Clark describes how Cui Jian became the voice of a new generation during the 1980s. His hit single "Nothing to my Name" (*yi wu suo you*) was part of the cultural fever that swept over China at that time. In this decade, poets, painters, movie makers, and musicians gathered together in soirees in the big cities of China to discuss the state of Chinese culture. A fascination for Western culture was translated into a critique on Chinese culture, as expressed, for example, in the television series *River Elegy* (*Heshang*) (for a discussion of the cultural fever (*wenhua re*) of the 1980s, see Wang 1996). The emergence of Cui Jian as a rock star needs to be read in this context of the rapid opening up of China. In his wake a vivid rock culture has emerged in China. This culture is often read in juxtaposition to the pop sounds that come from Hong Kong and Taiwan. The latter entered China also in the 1980s, most notably the Taiwanese pop star Teresa Teng (Deng Lijun). Whereas Cui Jian was sometimes banned for his provocative and political gestures, Teresa Teng was censored because of her overt expressions of sensuality.

Cui Jian is rightly seen as the godfather of Chinese rock culture. His husky voice, metaphorical lyrics, and cool appearance struck a chord with the youth of the 1980s and 1990s. Whereas many have read his work in an overtly political way, his work constitutes much more. In the words of Paul Clark:

> Cui himself consistently adopted an ambivalent attitude to politics that was not just a self-protective strategy. His songs were much more than politics, for the singer and his fans. They can be read as a deliberate attempt to put politics in its place, by making music out of wider, more personal issues of confusion and alienation. (2012: 109)

Cui Jian continues to perform, and branches out into other domains, like contemporary dance and cinema, and he was a music coach in the reality TV music show *China Star* (*zhongguo zhixing*) in the fall of 2015. Yet, his image remains tightly connected to the late 1980s and early 1990s. For many, his sound is a sound of nostalgia, of memories back to a time when change seemed possible, and the air was filled with dreams and hopes for a better future (Xu 2002). As we explained in the introduction, critique of the 1980s and 1990s generation is often packaged in references to the spirit of the 1980s. This is a quintessentially conservative framing, one that we can witness globally in which older generations critique the youth for being less engaged or less political or less creative, and instead more materialistic and individualistic than they used to be. As this book shows, also today's youth manage to carve out spaces of freedom and experimentation, and to blame a whole generation for being politically apathetic is as unjust as it is simplistic.

The early 1990s witnessed a second peak of alternative sounds, released under the Taiwanese label Magic Stone. The heavy metal of Tang Dynasty, the more ambient sound of Dou Wei, the folk music of Zhang Chu and the punky rebellious songs, combined with more sentimental ballads, of He Yong, managed to capture the audiences of China, Hong Kong, and Taiwan. After a short waning of enthusiasm during the mid-1990s, the later years in the 1990s are marked by a strong revival of Chinese rock music, with new bands popping up, exploring a wide range of styles, with local record companies like Modern Sky playing a pivotal role. This period marks a significant generational change, "Whereas in the early 1990s one could still speak of a *liumang* ('hooligan' or 'rascal') generation, around the turn of the century this had changed into the *dakou* generation, named after the cut CDs that were sold illegally on the streets of, among other cities, Beijing" (de Kloet 2005: 610).

It was in 1997 that we met rock singer Zuoxiao Zuzhou, in a small house close to the east gate of Peking University. At that time, as the vocalist of the underground band NO, his haunted, high-pitched voice stood out, maneuvering him to the margins of Chinese rock culture. Zuoxiao Zuzhou has from the beginning of his career operated on the boundaries of rock culture and the artistic circles of Beijing, where he was a member of the Beijing East Village Art collective. His strong links with artists Ai Weiwei, Meng Jinghui, and filmmaker Jia Zhangke, among many others, have made him a special figure in the Beijing rock scene. Remarkably, his fame increased significantly after 2008, his sound became more mellow, and he became much more like a star figure or, better, a cult hero, being the closing act of large-scale festivals and frequently featuring in the news together with Ai Weiwei as well as Han Han.

We can read his increased popularity as a sign that contemporary Chinese youth are interested in socially engaged sounds, but as Jeroen Groenewegen-Lau argues in his article devoted to the work of Zuoxiao Zuzhou, "Zuoxiao owes this success to humour and parody, and a turn towards a less pointed social critique and a more hedonistic sound. As such, this recent success engages with a larger cultural trend in which youngsters cynically participate in the status quo" (2011). Groenewegen-Lau quotes Zuoxiao from his autobiography where he explains his attitude towards politics:

> Even if I want to oppose something I won't depend on external forces. I am just an individual, expressing intuitive, emotional things. I wrote on Temple Fair Tour: "you already act, to be at ease. Being at ease is freedom. Freedom is a Human Right. But Human Rights are politics! Comrade, you have stumbled upon the stage of politics." Artists have a hard time really understanding politics. I think Bob Dylan and Bono don't even get it. But when others listen to your songs and read your lyrics, they will tell you that you're political. (Groenewegen-Lau 2011)

In an interview he explained to us how he gradually moved away from his intellectual style. He explained (in 2008):

I'm more direct now. I used to fall in the track of these stupid intellectuals, now I don't give a damn to the so-called being "artistic." I don't care about choosing the "right words."

Zuoxiao Zuzhou is a quite exceptional rock singer, one of the few that continues to operate on the boundaries of the politically permissible, and his becoming a cult hero shows that also socially engaged rock can appeal to contemporary Chinese youth. That his style, his lyrics, and his music are full of parody and irony makes him more difficult to grasp, which strengthens his star persona. Like the New Pants, humor plays an important role in his music; you never know if he is really serious. Zuoxiao Zuzhou allows Chinese youth to engage in social critique that remains within the boundaries of the permissible, which may not directly undermine the status quo of Chinese society, but it at least pokes fun at it.

The opening up of China's media culture, in conjunction with the emergence of a more affluent generation of young Chinese, has radically altered the mediascape of China. Whereas in the late 1990s, rock concerts generally took place in small bars, by now, large-scale rock festivals have become a yearly ritual. The Strawberry Festival that takes place in the outskirts of Beijing, and has also versions in other cities in China, now attracts thousands of young people. For the generation from the 1980s and the 1990s, rock has become not so much a niche subculture, but rather a lifestyle choice, a scene one dives into during the May holidays, to return back to study or work a few days later, while in the evening watching the latest version of *I Am a Singer* on Hunan TV.

As we explained earlier, rock is driven by what can be termed the rock mythology, a discourse through which rock, in contrast to pop, is constructed as rebellious, authentic, masculine, and loud (de Kloet 2010). We indicated how rock bands always face the threat of being labeled as mere copycats, at most bleak and outdated imitations of the

West. This may well explain why in the past many bands were eager to incorporate Chinese elements into their music, ranging from the *guzheng* in Cui Jian's songs, to the reference back to dynastic times in Tang Dynasty, the Beijing-like singing voice of Qiu Ye in the music of the band Zi Yue, the gender-bending performances that bring to mind the Beijing opera of Second Hand Rose, the ethnic style of Mongolian rockers Hanggai, and the appropriations of the communist past by Cui Jian. However, since the 2000s it seems fair to claim that bands care less about being Chinese or not, they more easily adopt a cosmopolitan style, sing in English, and do not shy away from making references to their sources of inspiration. The band Reestablishing the Rights of Statues (RETROS), for example, refer to the UK post-punk band Bauhaus as an important source of inspiration, and the Carsick Cars were keen to play as the support act when Sonic Youth played in Beijing. This increased cosmopolitanization of Chinese youth culture can be traced on many levels, not only in music, but also in cinema (see chapter 4), literature, and fashion, as we have already seen.

This leaves us with an interesting paradox: while Chinese youth seem to care less about Chineseness in media consumption and lifestyle, they simultaneously are often vivid supporters of a Chinese nationalism. Nevertheless, their support of the nation-state comes with patterns of cultural production and consumption that clearly go beyond the boundaries of the same nation-state. We consequently see a surprising fusion of patriotism and cosmopolitanism that characterizes contemporary Chinese youth culture. This alludes to a conceptually mistaken juxtaposition: patriotism and cosmopolitanism are not each other's opposite, but rather, they are intimately intertwined, or in the words of Ulrich Beck, "we need roots in order to have wings" (2002: 19).

Whereas the performances in small bars are frequented by a relatively small group of rock fans, the bigger stadium concerts of, for example, Second Hand Rose manage to attract thousands of people.

It is in particular the rock festivals that constitute the epicenter of today's rock culture. These are when thousands of fans from all over China flock to the big metropolis to see their bands perform. "From some 10 large-scale open-air festivals in 2007, the number increased to about 40 festivals by 2010" (Groenewegen-Lau 2014: 7). It is tempting to give these festivals a political reading; several times the authorities have banned them. And there is a critical edge to RETROS singing out loud "Hang the Police" while the police keep the audience under control. Similarly, the video that was shown during a performance by Zuoxiao Zuzhou in 2010 at the Strawberry Festival on the outskirts of Beijing stirred up the audience. Again the police kept them under control, yet on screen they were offered fragments from the Ai Weiwei documentary *Let Feng Zhenghu Go Home* (2009). Feng is a Chinese economist and human rights writer and blogger who left China in April 2009 for medical treatment in Japan after being jailed for 41 days in Shanghai without official explanation. In June 2009 he attempted to return to China but was refused entry. After eight unsuccessful attempts, he refused to leave the immigration hall in Narita Airport. In February 2010 he managed to return to Shanghai where he stayed under house arrest. The audience instantly recognized these fragments during the performance, and started to applaud and cheer loudly. This combination of a clearly articulated political critique among a crowd that was so visibly under the control of the police attests to the complexities and contradictions of the possibility for doing politics in China. It also suggests a latent political danger to the regime if the current context is altered to allow for such an open critique.

Moments like these are what Groenewegen-Lau (2014) calls "utopian moments"; they lie at the heart of music festivals. He provides an example from the performance by Miserable Faith in the MIDI Music Festival of 2010, during which the audience shouted along with the band's classic bearing the Maoist-cum-Foucauldian title "Whenever There's Oppression, There's Resistance" (Groenewegen-Lau 2014:

Image 3. Queen Sea Big Shark perform at the 2016 Strawberry Music Festival (photo by Jeroen de Kloet)

3). Interestingly, this was also the song the band performed in the fall of 2015 on the reality show *China Star* (*Zhongguo zhixing*) at the invitation of coach Cui Jian. When we attended the recording at the studios of Shanghai Television on Monday, December 7, 2015, we were amazed to see the audience sing along with such a provocative line, and wondered: how can this be on TV? However, when *China Star* was broadcast a few days later, the song was indeed deleted from the show. Yet, during the voting process at the end of the program, the band had to leave the show as they received the lowest score from the jury and the audience. So the television audience was presented with the bizarre case of watching a band receiving a low score for their performance without seeing the actual performance. The censored clip soon appeared online on *Weibo*, making it possible for the audiences to still check it out – attesting to the schism between official media and online spaces in China.

Back to the rock festival: just as it is too easy to read the cosmopolitanization of Chinese youth culture as contradicting patriotic sentiments, so should one avoid reading music festivals solely as places of political protest. As we have shown, at certain times and certain places, political dissent does get articulated, and the banning of the 2015 edition of the Strawberry Festival, as well as numerous instances in the past when festivals were cancelled just before they were about to start, shows how authorities do consider them sensitive events. But as Groenewegen-Lau shows in his analysis of music festivals, such a political reading of these festivals ignores the complex entanglement between the state and the cultural industries in China. Groenewegen-Lau shows how in the first decade of the 2000s, bands started to earn a lot for their performances: by 2001, a performance by Miserable Faith could earn the band a fee between RMB 50,000 and RMB 100,000. Groenewegen-Lau quotes organizer Shen Lihui stating:

> The last couple of years a lot of bands earned over a million a year. Accounts are easy to settle. For instance if thirty of the fifty music festivals book you and you earn thirty to fifty thousand a show, you'll make more than a million. Only now they've become rock stars. In the past they were rock aspirants. Stars are wealthy because of the market. Only then they can perform for years without disbanding. (2014: 5)

Groenewegen-Lau shows how city governments started to support festivals financially as part of their city branding tactics. Thus, the rise of the creative industry and creative city discourse in China since the mid-2000s has changed the way authorities view music festivals. They now come to brand the creative and hip city. In their attempt to move from a "Made in China" to a "Created in China" country (Keane 2013), China is strongly promoting its creative cultures.

Whereas contemporary art used to be a quite sensitive domain, by now it is showcased in creative districts like 798 in Beijing, attesting to the alleged openness of contemporary China. Music festivals can be seen in a similar light, just as the state now also sends Chinese rock bands abroad as part of their soft power policies. The state, the market, and the music people are thus involved in complex negotiations over the production of youth culture in China. Yet, despite this complex entanglement, one that we can also see in the media world at large in China, we contend with Groenewegen-Lau that "despite its disavowal of politics, Modern Sky [the organizer of the Strawberry Festival] empowers audience and bands, and offers youngsters a heterotopia or alternative space, transcending pressures to conform within the family, the educational system, and the workplace" (2014: 25). Groenewegen-Lau quotes vocalist Gao Hu of Miserable Faith who claims that:

> Yes, maybe music festivals have become a kind of entertainment. But I still think rock music can provide temporary utopias. Maybe you have to spend more energy to find something that moves you, you have to go out and discover, not stand back and let the music overwhelm you (Gao Hu, personal communication, April 2012). (Groenewegen-Lau 2014: 26)

As we show throughout this book, the juxtaposition between entertainment and utopia needs to be questioned; instead, it makes more sense to think of utopian *moments*, and thus to insert a stronger sense of time and space into the analysis. Music festivals, rock concerts, and music releases, they all offer moments of change, they can constitute what can be termed temporal utopian moments that are pregnant with a commitment to change and difference. These are carnivalesque moments during which Chinese youth experiment with alternatives, without necessarily pursuing them in everyday life.

DIGITAL STYLES

In June 2015, China had 668 million Internet users, and the Internet penetration reached 48.8 percent; the number of mobile Internet users in China reached 594 million, and mobile netizens accounted for 88.9 percent of the total netizen population (CNNIC 2015: 1). Internet penetration is highest in urban areas among those aged 10–19 (85.1 percent), 20–29 (85.1 percent) and 30–39 (74.7 percent) (CNNIC 2015: 9). In her study on youth and the Internet, Liu observes that "the vast majority of my informants employed the Internet mainly or purely for entertainment....Chinese youth seem to employ the Net for entertainment to a greater extent than their counterparts in some Western societies" (2013: 181). We share a similar observation, and like Liu, we link this desire for entertainment to the pressures Chinese youth face as discussed before. The most popular use of new technologies is instant messaging (CNNIC 2015: 22), which has resulted in funny movies on the Internet in which a circle of friends during dinner only gaze at their mobile phones. Among the 90s generation, the phrase "collective loneliness" (*quntixing gudu*) has emerged. A study quotes Dong, a 24-year-old female newspaper editor in Wuhan, saying:

> When it comes to hanging out together, I think people should talk and laugh when they get together in a restaurant or KTV. But now everyone is controlled by his or her cell phone. Everyone just keeps looking at a phone. It is not easy to hang out together. But I don't know what we are doing. So when we hang out together now, the first thing is to collect everyone's phone. Nobody is allowed to play with a phone during the meeting. (Yiguanzhiku and Tengxun 2014: 60)

We have started our discussion on new media with these mundane everyday uses, but these uses also have wider social and political implications. Before we explore these, for example by analyzing Internet memes in which entertainment and politics converge, we will first briefly theorize the relation between technology and society.

We can trace a curious and quite contradictory way in which new media in China are generally discussed, in particular in journalistic discourse: either the Internet in China is seen as a force for freedom bringing political change, or it is read as a tool for increased surveillance and control (Yang 2011). The danger in such assertions is a falling back into a technological determinism, in which technologies are interpreted as something outside society, and as something that has an independent but direct influence on society (Williams 2003). But technology and society are intertwined, they are mutually constitutive, as becomes clear when we see how the workings of the Internet in China are different from the workings of the Internet in, say, the United States. Just as the interface of *Weibo* is not the same as the interface of Twitter, and both are constantly evolving, this allows for different modes of interaction and sharing. We are thus wary of statements like "*Weibo* will promote democratic change in China," as if the platform operates as a force independent from society. Similarly, we prefer to steer away from its opposite, and read *Weibo* purely as the technological outcome of social processes. Following Raymond Williams, and in his slipstream theorists from the social construction of technology approach like Wiebe Bijker (1997) and actor network theory from Bruno Latour (1987) – approaches that all have distinct, different, and at times contradictory angles, but that share with us a deep mistrust of technological determinism – we read both as mutually constitutive.

We contend that the affordances of new technologies – as shaped by, but also as a changing force of, society – allow for political moments, just as they increase control over people. When we add "youth" to this discourse, we can also trace in the literature a strong pathologizing discourse on addiction to the Internet and to online gaming. Rather than asking ourselves what the Internet does to youth, we prefer to complicate this question, and wonder how youth and new media have become entangled in everyday practices. This has changed swiftly over the past decade. Starting in the early 2000s with the BBS (bulletin board system) platforms, then moving to blogs, to today's culture of *Weibo* and Wechat, the digital sphere in China has changed profoundly, like it has elsewhere. The Internet is quite tightly censored in China, involving even what is termed the "50 cents army" – people who write comments in favor of the Party and get paid for that by the Party. Netizens even invented their own word and character – *wao* – to refer to them. The army did not work too well: "pro-government postings have become so repetitive and mechanical that Web users have little trouble spotting them" (Link and Qiang 2013: 91). Many sites are blocked, including Facebook and Twitter, but these social networks do get a Chinese version, like the moments option in Wechat instead of Facebook and *Weibo* instead of Twitter. These platforms are, however, closely monitored, turning them into tools of surveillance as well. The technologically savvy youth have a VPN account that allows them to circumvent what is termed the Great Firewall of China. Many have more than one VPN account, as sometimes the system manages to block these as well.

In our experience, the slow speed of Internet in China may well be the most successful mode of censorship: all the downloading and sharing takes patience. According to the Akamai ranking, China's average connection speed in 2015 was 3.7 MB/s, compared to 13 for the UK, 15.8 for Hong Kong and 20.5 for the number one on the list, South Korea (Wikipedia 2015). In a survey in 2008 among urban youth, 52.4 percent indicate being very unsatisfied or unsatisfied about not getting access to all websites, 24.5 percent felt it is quite understandable, and 18.9 percent claimed not to care (Guo and Wu 2009: 22). Censorship is thus troublesome, yet it has also become a matter of fact in everyday life. The authorities do also try to give it a better face. The aesthetics of censorship are like the character that one can find in public spaces. It can happen that while you are chatting, the

Internet police comes walking onto your screen to show you are being watched. The image used for these characters clearly resembles Japanese anime characters. With their big eyes, they connote cuteness, rather than surveillance, and thus help to make the system appear innocent. The globalization of Japanese anime thus produces a quite specific appropriation by the Chinese authorities, helping them to update their aesthetics, and turn censorship into a *kawaii* affair.

Censorship in China is also a creative force. First, from a more philosophical angle, censorship actually produces that which it aims to silence, by uttering the words and issues that one should not speak about, one cannot help but already articulate them. Thus, by deeming the June 4 "incident" to be a sensitive issue, or the Nobel Prize for Liu Xiaobo, the authorities actually help direct attention toward both events (see Butler 1997). Second, as a creative force, it inspires the proliferation of all kinds of tactics that help evade the system. For example, an empty chair became the symbol for Liu Xiaobo, gesturing toward his detainment, because of which he could not attend the ceremony to receive his prize in Oslo.

Memes are another domain to play around with the censors, and they have become a joyful playground for Chinese netizens to express what cannot be expressed. Memes – in Chinese referred to also as *e'gao* or online spoofs – are part of what Jenkins has termed a "participatory culture," in which people jointly produce, combine, and circulate content and make connections among dispersed media content (Jenkins 2006). "Fundamental to this complex web is the practice of reconfiguring content and publicly displaying it in parodies, mashups, remixes and other derivative formats" (Shifman 2011: 188). Memes turn consumers into producers, and popular culture constitutes the raw material that is, with the help of digital technologies, used and reappropriated and turned into new content.

Examples of memes from China are endless. Two of the most prominent examples come from the Story of a Bun and the Backdorm Boys.

The Story of a Bun was a mashup directed against the 2005 movie *The Promise (Wu Ji)* by Chen Kaige. Thirty-one-year-old sound engineer Hu Ge produced a 20-minute long video spoof titled *A Bloody Case over a Steamed Bun* turning the fantasy story into a crime story. The satire quickly went viral. In it he makes fun of the movie, and its self-orientalizing aesthetics, and thus of Chen Kaige, but also of typical-style CCTV reporting, and it engages with social problems like China's intense commercialization (Meng 2011). As Meng writes, "by mixing together images from a highly commercialized costume drama with the typical discursive style of the official news media, while making constant reference to contemporary social problems, Hu Ge successfully creates a comic yet subversive text that ridicules the establishment" (2011: 42). The Backdorm Boys reached national, and to some extent, global fame after their mimicry of the Backstreet Boys. We see two boys in a student dorm mimicking the band, while a third is sitting in front of his computer screen. Following the success of this video, they started to mimic more bands, such as the German band Trio and their 1980s classic "Da Da Da," during the World Cup of 2006. The Backdorm Boys attest to the possibility of the Internet as a place where one can create one's own stardom and negotiate a new sensibility of authenticity, one that resides in the humorous and the banal, rather than the tragic and the serious (de Kloet and Teurlings 2008). However, one has to be careful in celebrating this potential. Research shows that only few users make content, most remain consumers, and there is little reason to think that this will be different in the case of China (van Dijck 2013).

Two examples with a strong political connotation are the grass-mud horse and the River Crab, both of which went viral in 2009, the year China tightened its Internet control. The grass-mud horse, or *caonima*, is a homophone for "fuck your mother." A video appeared online, "Song of the Grass-Mud Horse," in which a cheerful song is performed, with children's voices, while we see some cute grazing alpacas on the grasslands. "This seemingly innocuous composition of the infantile and the pastoral is a tour de force display of netizen populism, larded with dirty puns and political in-jokes that are easily decoded but still give the viewer a sense of participation in a subversive escapade" (Rea 2013: 161; see also Link and Qiang 2013). To give just a few lines from the lyrics (from Rea 2013: 162), while we can read "On the vast and beautiful Ma-le Gobi desert is a herd of grass-mud horses," an alternative reading is "In your mother's vast and beautiful cunt is a group fucking your mother." The sentence "To graze on the grass and not be eaten, they defeated the river crabs," means "To fuck and not be eaten, they defeated the 'harmonizing' censors."

For audiences, there is tremendous pleasure in decoding such hidden messages, and soon the grass-mud horse could be found on all corners of the Internet as well as offline, in raps, poetry, visual art, illustrations, T-shirts, and other merchandise. The reference to the river crab points to another symbol that went viral. In Chinese, river crab is pronounced as *hexie*, a homophone for harmony. China's policy toward a harmonious society, one that has under Xi Jinping been replaced by the China Dream, is used to legitimize censorship policies. Hence numerous river crabs circulate on the Internet, some with expensive golden watches, signifying the practice of bribery. What these examples show is how Chinese youth are engaged in a playful cut-and-paste game in which they borrow from different cultural sources, both local and global, to construct new meanings. In the words of Rea, "*e'gao* may well be considered yet another expression of the 'banal cosmopolitanism' – a mindset that takes for granted a globalized everyday experience – that sociologists have shown to be more salient than national differences in determining consumer responses to global media texts" (2013: 169). What, in Rea's view, makes them different from Western examples of participatory culture are linguistic, discursive, material, and political factors.

The examples so far reveal a humorous world with memes and other forms of parody of the Party. When reading the overview of political contention on the Internet by Yang Guobin, we can see that activism is not the privilege of the young only. He traces a genealogy toward the past and the revolutionary zeal of the Red Guards when he writes that "online activism is emblematic of a long revolution unfolding in China today, a revolution intertwining cultural, social, and political transformations. The main manifestations of these transformations are cultural creativity, civic engagement and organizing, and citizens' unofficial democracy" (Yang 2011: 24). This account inspires him to the quite optimistic conclusion that "The effervescence of online contention, as part of China's new citizen activism, indicates the palpable revival of the revolutionary impulse in Chinese society. The power of the Internet lies in revealing this impulse and showing the ever stronger aspirations for a more just and democratic society" (Yang 2011: 24).

While we acknowledge with Yang that the Internet has changed Chinese society deeply, we are less sure about his optimistic reading. First, the link he makes with China's past, a connection also drawn by Clark (2012), runs the danger of turning the Internet into a platform with unique Chinese characteristics. This not only smacks of cultural essentialism, it also tends to ignore the profound global entanglements on different levels (development of technologies, contents, users, etc.). Second, his model allows little reflection on, or ascribes no agency to, the workings of technology. Third, whereas Yang rightly observes that the uses of the Internet more often than not conflate with the Party, or even amplify them, for example in the rise of popular nationalist movements online, he tends not to include these uses, nor to reflect further upon the power of control and surveillance digital technologies hold. The rise of youthful online popular nationalism since 2000 was expressed in different protests directed against Japan or the United

States – producing the specific term "Internet nationalism" (*wangluo minzuzhuyi*) (Clark 2012: 168).

Obviously, many public discussions on online cultures focus on China's most popular social media sites *Weixin* and Sina *Weibo*, with 355 million and 129 million users respectively, according to figures released by Tencent in 2014 (Yiguanzhiku and Tengxun 2014). The former, also known as Wechat, is rapidly gaining popularity, at the expense of *Weibo* (Z. Wang 2015). A quite spectacular scene of youth online consumption can be observed in almost every university and residential district. In all big cities, including Beijing, Shanghai, and Guangzhou, when we walk out of the main university gates and some of the private residential districts (*xiaoqu*), there will be small vans of Shunfeng (SF), Yuantong (YTO), and Zhongtong Express (ZTO) docking with staff loading off small parcels. Arrays of parcels are lined up on the pedestrian areas where students and youngsters come from their own university and residential districts to search and pick up their own parcels ordered online through various shopping sites. Such express delivery systems together with the online shopping sites then form the basis where youth are connected to the global world through consumption practices.

The availability of online shopping sites, in addition to access to websites overseas and local portals that carry foreign information, precipitates and accelerates the formation of a "global youth culture." But the consumption sites in China tend to sell a potpourri of Western goods, locally made products faking Western goods, and local commodities imitating others from without. The best example is *Taobao*, the largest online shop in China. With the burgeoning online shopping consumption, from individual private owner *gaoti*, to chain shops, they all join this gold rush in China. Then, *Taobao* becomes a synchronic warehouse of different modalities of consumerist modernity. The young consumers will look for trendy products from Korea, Japan and the West. In the rush to gain a market share, many online shops do their utmost to strike an international and cosmopolitan image. *Taobao* operates like a desiring machine, it is part of what can be termed a banal cosmopolitan consumption culture, which is anachronistically extracted from that weird mixture of a global market economy and a socialist nation-state.

While the Internet allows Chinese youth to experiment online with new identities, new alliances, new consumption habits, and new forms of politics, at the same time, their online work may not only be mined for commercial purposes, they can also be much more easily traced by the authorities. Global concerns over the commercialization of the Internet, the political economy behind platforms like Twitter, YouTube and Facebook and privacy infringement (see van Dijck 2013) may be even more urgent in the context of China. Rather than focusing solely on the issue of censorship, these wider forms of digital exploitation, manipulation, and surveillance are becoming more urgent foci of research when studying Chinese youth and new media. Yang also writes about this in the afterword of his book, when he points at "the growing sophistication of the state's Internet governance strategies and the more pervasive influence of commercial interests" (2011: 233).

One aspect of digital cultures that we have not yet discussed is their ability to create a public and make someone famous outside the working of the mainstream media. Bloggers like Wang Xiaofeng, Michael Anti, and Zuola and also Sister Hibiscus have been prolific opinion makers in China. A term has emerged for these Internet celebrities: they are called Big V (*da-V*), with the V referring to VIP, and at times they have used their power to mobilize people. For example, Zuola helped trigger street protests in Xiamen against a chemical factory. Probably the best example of someone whose fame is directly linked to the power of the Internet is Han Han. Indeed, racing driver, blogger, writer, and cultural entrepreneur Han Han owes much of his fame not only to his good looks, but also to the Internet. His blogs have appeared as a book – a common practice in China – that has been translated into different languages. Like Zuoxiao Zuzhou, Han Han manages perfectly well to balance on the tightrope between what can and what cannot be said. He, as a school dropout, became famous through a novel on the examination pressure on high school students. "Such was his celebrity by 2008, he was able to make sarcastic comments on official discourse and relatively sensitive political matters on his blog while escaping much censure from the authorities. Fame and fandom put Han Han above the law to a degree that only the Internet could allow" (Clark 2012: 159). After he published three essays on revolution, democracy, and freedom in December 2011, audiences were disappointed in him given the conservative stance he expressed. This disappointment soon morphed into a scandal when "a well-known Internet user, Maitian, argued that Han Han's blogs were not, or at least not entirely, written by himself, but by a 'team'. A commercial logic was suspected behind this theory, as it would allow Han Han to be so enormously productive in different fields" (Poell et al. 2014: 8). This development attests to the potential of the Internet to make and break reputations. In the end, however, Han Han managed to secure his reputation and he remains one of China's most prolific cultural entrepreneurs.

CONCLUSION

The assertion that globalization produces a homogeneous culture in China has been debunked in this chapter. Our analysis of fashion styles, music styles, and digital styles shows that they all operate as important domains through which Chinese youth experiment with different identities, different lifestyles, different embodiments. These can be politically sensitive styles, but if these are played out, it is mostly in a specific place at a specific moment. Chinese youth culture, as Paul Clark rightly observes, "cannot be understood through mapping phenomena according to grid patterns of simple binaries: Chinese and Western, local and global, or traditional and modern. The developments were more complex and also spontaneous, ungoverned, uneven, and unpredictable" (2012: 192). The developments are above all more entangled; the global is always already implicated in the local, just as the digital and the non-digital, or online and offline, are enmeshed in one another.

The possibilities for Chinese youth to experiment with different styles have expanded exponentially over the past two decades. This does not entail necessarily more freedom; on the contrary, as we have seen, the Internet also allows for a much closer mode of surveillance, and is also governed by a deeply commercial logic. The paradox of China may well be that despite its rapid opening up, despite its astounding economic growth, despite the emergence of a China Dream, modes of control seem to have intensified rather than diminished. This intensification of power – from the state–cultural industry nexus – increasingly operates like a Foucauldian mode of biopower, a power that penetrates deep into the body, that produces individuality as its mode of operation. Therefore we are not univocally celebrating the proliferation of difference in Chinese youth culture, as this production of difference (expressed in style, expressed through consumption) has not only a commercial logic underpinning it, but also a governmental one. It produces a specific citizenry, one that is youthful, that is allowed to play around, to make funny memes, to dance to Carsick Cars' aggressive song "Zhongnanhai" – a metaphorical reference to the June 4 student protest movement – one that dresses up in funky styles that get their inspiration from traditional Chinese attire as well as form the most recent Japanese fashion, yet all these markers of distinction, of difference, also help to contain, to make visible, to control.

<table>
<tr><td>

3

</td><td>

Localization of
Regional Culture

</td></tr>
</table>

Value the time of youthfulness, pleasure is not desired

Wen Tianxiang (1236–1283)

INTRODUCTION

Wen Tianxiang was one of the very few patriotic scholar-generals in the last days of the Song Dynasty against the intruders, the Mongols and the Khan. He chose to die rather than to surrender and betray his own country. As a constructing block of righteousness in Chinese history, Wen's narrative suggests that in the valuable time of being young, blind pursuit of pleasure is not what a man of vital importance would want to do. Ostensibly his ideal is against today's socialist market economy of China, which largely hinges on profit, consumption, and desire. Under the wheels of capitalism, Chinese have become one of the main consumers, and not only domestically, they are indeed (in)famous for global consumption wherever they go. Louis Vuitton shops in Paris have long queues of predominantly Chinese customers waiting outside the shop for their turn. The D&G store in Hong Kong that was once said to serve only Chinese tourists became international news. Peculiar to youth consumption, youngsters are the strategic target of popular brands (Carah 2010), from materialistic consumption of, among others, mobile phones (e.g. iPhones and Samsung), computers (e.g. Mac computers and iPads), fashion (e.g. A&F and

Gap), food and drink (e.g. Coca-Cola, Starbucks, and McDonald's), to cultural consumption including movies, American TV dramas, Western and K-pop music, and games. In the wake of the desiring machine called global capitalism, the importance of pleasure is growing and capitalized on through a constant flow of commodities and values. Discussed in this chapter is the Chinese youngsters' desire as reflected in their cultural consumption of localized contents of regional cultural flows. Such individual desire for something from without is overtly connected to a potpourri of values, from class consciousness, consumerism, fetishism to liberalism, democracy, and of course regional and global values. While in this chapter we do not attempt to predict the possible consequences of, or attribute concrete effects to, such consumption, we do claim that their aspiration of non-local, regional consumption and content indexes their values and beliefs in contemporary China.

An important footnote to our argument, however, is that Chinese youth's cultural consumption of these localized regional contents does not necessarily lead to a celebration of values from without, and there are always disjunctures between regional values and their mutations in localized content. As we described in chapter 2, global culture or globalization in China is a deeply disjointed globalization in which only certain cultural elements are able to be imported into China for broadcasting and circulation (Fung 2008b). In this chapter, we continue to complicate this argument. Chapter 2 focuses on the cultural effect of imported global cultural products within the territory of China after censorship, understood as including vigorous processes of blocking and filtering. In this chapter, what is emphasized is the reproduction, replication, or localization of the regional, inter-Asian global forms in China (Chua 2012). In other words, we add another layer of cultural translation: it is not only the version of global culture that is allowed to be seen in mainland China; there is also a desirable and localized regional culture. Then, the questions discussed are not whether youth share the regional values or how much they do. What is intellectually intriguing is more about how these values are localized. Who localizes them? What Chinese enterprises have learned and replicated the strategies to sell culture to domestic Chinese youth? What does this tell us about contemporary Chinese youth?

At this point, we are not interested in whether youth or some youth are able to offer resistance to these localized versions of the regional, which is a core concern of cultural studies (for a critique on the idea of critique and resistance in cultural studies, see Morris 1988 and Illouz 2007). Neither do we want to simply condemn consumption as something bad nor pleasure as insignificant, as we have already argued in previous chapters. Here, we extend our discussion in chapter 2 and examine how regional culture, particularly Japanese and Korean pop culture, could be localized and infiltrated into China that in turn produces scripts for youth to recreate more space for themselves.

As discussed in earlier chapters, in recognition of the potential of growing dissent of Chinese society as a consequence of corruption, unequal development, and social inequality, there is the argument that the state co-produces with global capital to mold popular culture in such a way that it is not incompatible with the state agenda (Fung, 2008a). In this chapter, we rather focus on localized-regional-popular culture that is not directly reproduced by the state but by capitals and markets that are relatively – but never completely – autonomous from the state. In some cases, it is localization in formal and legal ways, while others are cultural imitations, cloning the cultural forms from a certain country without a clear direct source. Besides, such expression, representation, and production impinges upon not only global culture and resources, but builds on variations of culture, including Japanese and Korean culture as constructed, appropriated, and limited by the state within China. Different from the state-dictated domains – politics, family, and education – and domestically produced cultural domains, the relatively autonomous localized regional culture, on the one hand,

Image 4. Youth flocking to the cinema to watch Hollywood movies in 2016 (photo by Anthony Fung)

allows for a wider range of negotiation and maneuvering, and, on the other, creates new cultural forms in China hitherto unseen.

But how are such regional cultural forms translated and marketed to Chinese youth? Generally lacking local or alternative space, how could these localized cultures be impactful in China? Building upon the arguments in the earlier chapters, this chapter describes such translated or locally developed but regionally cloned, emerging cultural forms that facilitate youth to own individual and small spaces. These new localized forms, operations, and organizations of popular culture inaugurate a new kind of popular culture that the state has not seen before and therefore could not find the right vocabulary to ban or censor it, at least, during the initial phase when it grows and spreads. In the following, we will first outline CCTV's value management in adopting global TV formats and class re-imagination in the Chinese version of a regional TV drama *Meteor Garden*. We will then examine the increasing import of regional formats such as *Running Man* and the turn to gamification as well as the cultural space they open up. We conclude by way of pop music, where we argue for the emergence of new, regionally informed, girl and boy groups such as SNH48 and TFBoys, their fandom practices, and political significance. We do so against a context where the older generation of Chinese pop idols, for instance Jay Chou and Li Yuchun, often works in tandem with the state–market nexus.

LOCALIZING TV FORMAT FROM WITHOUT

Parts of these newly developed forms are still connected to the state ideological apparatus. Commercialization of television slowly accelerated the globalization of China's TV programming in the sense that many provincial and city stations started to clone foreign programs in the mid-1990s. After 2000, more legal TV format franchises were seen on Chinese television stations (Keane et al. 2007). The latter is part of the global trade in TV formats; this involves a trading of the so-called "blue book" with the rules and regulations attached to the format, and subsequent localization of the design and packaging of an idea of television production from overseas.

One of the earliest examples is a CCTV remake of the French version of *Between Cities*, a sport and game show that was premiered in October 1998. The program, emphasizing the spirit of fair competition, is a way not only to promote a city but also fills a gap in entertaining programming among all the serious propaganda on CCTV. In the same year, CCTV used 4 million RMB to localize GO BINGO's *Who Wants to be a Millionaire* to produce *Lucky 52* (*Xingyun 52*) and later in 2000 *Happy Dictionary* (*Kaixin Zidian*). According to our interview with the producer, the localized version on the one hand has to take care of the audience's wishes, and on the other serves to pitch family values. The latter is a core mission of national television. Offering a million as the selling point of the original television format naturally means an excessive monetary incentive. Thus, instead, winners in the Chinese version are given electric appliances of a much lower value. In these early adoptions of global television formats, we witness a high synchronization with the state's ideology, allowing very little room for imagination or negotiation. Soon after CCTV's pioneering case, TV format adoption began to flood China.

CCTV's case shows that the authorities have taken a proactive role in bringing global products to China. But it also suggests that this globalization process is under the state's supervision and monitoring. Through their mediating role, the Chinese authorities are able to package political ideals into commercial cultural forms by means of modifying overseas television formats. Rather than directly suppressing the influence and influx of global cultural products and capital, the Chinese state-owned stations acted as the filters censoring content that advocates values such as freedom, democracy, and, like the case above, earning easy money. When these "missions" are decentralized in provincial and city television channels, coupled to the economic logic of these television formats, the nature of the adoption has changed.

Given that the notion of intellectual property protection is not strong in China, many of the TV format adoptions have been imitations of television programs (Moran 1998). The most widely cloned TV format is probably the highly popular US program *Survivor*, which in turn derives from the Swedish television series *Expedition Robinson*

(1997). Known versions of *Survivor* in China include *I Shouldn't Be Alive* produced by Guangdong TV, *Canon Survival Camp* by Guizhou TV (2002), and the cable TV's *Go into Shangri-la* by Beijing Vhand Culture Communication (2001). While *Survivor* targeted the younger generation – thus a stronger accent on individualism in the form of competition rather than on family values – the Chinese versions largely toe the Party line. These early cloning examples seek to reduce the "impact" of the program by playing down the fierce rivalry among the participants and resetting the focus on the competition between human beings and their environment. At the same time, certain components of the program reiterate and reify national values of the PRC in subtle ways. For instance, the voting mechanism in the original format is scrapped. At the same time, *Canon Survival Camp* cherishes collective effort and public virtues over personal interest, full of compassion and team leadership (Keane et al. 2007). In sum, although the Chinese stations brought more cosmopolitan formats into China, the core values of the programs do not depart radically from other censored contents. This goes back to our earlier argument that "globalization" processes in relation to youth might result in something quite different than might be expected. While the adaptation of program formats in television systems across the globe has become a regular and common media strategy for TV stations (Moran 1998), what the state and its ideological apparatus in China are doing is to turn such adoptions to their advantage.

REGIONAL TV FORMATS AND CLASS RE-IMAGINATION

Ten years after the TV format purchase, however, there are remarkable changes to localization of television. First, increasingly, there is a cultural localization of TV programs that aim to reach youth, different from earlier programs that targeted more a family and general audience. Second, apart from the usual practice of adopting a Western TV format, cloning, circulation, and franchising of television or idol-making formats from Korea and Japan has become much more prominent in the stations' drive to attract the youth audience. In addition to their cultural proximity, the general popularity of Korean and Japanese culture in the region also explains why cultural forms from these areas are appropriated. In the case of the Korean format, there is also the push force from Korea as the export of cultural product fosters soft power. This phenomenon is usually referred to as an inter-Asian cultural flow (Chua 2004, 2012; Fung 2007), and in this chapter, instead of the import—export aspect, we focus more on these flows, and on how these Asian cultures are localized.

The first example is *Meteor Garden*, a comic that originates from Japan, written and illustrated by Yoko Kamio. The plot is about a love story happening among four boys from well-off families and a girl with poor family background but who somehow ends up studying in the same elite high school. The comic was then adapted into four versions of TV dramas: in Taiwan, Japan, South Korea and China. *Meteor Garden* was first produced as an idol drama in Taiwan in 2001. The TV drama achieved huge commercial success with a minimum of 500 million viewers across Asia. F4, the four boys in the drama, also gained popularity and created a "Young-Boy-Idol" group trend in Taiwan, which soon spread over Asia. During that time, F4 were so popular in China that the four boy idols became the promoters of major global brands in China.

The same TV format was later adapted by South Korea (named *Boys Over Flowers*), Japan (also named *Boys Over Flowers*) and finally China (named *Let's Go Watch the Meteor Shower*). As AGB Nelson reported, the audience for *Boys Over Flowers* are primarily women aged 15–22. The Chinese version, *Let's Go Watch the Meteor Shower*, broadcast in 2009 and 2010 by Hunan TV, became the number one TV drama after a week of its broadcasting. All these versions achieved ratings and economic success among the youth market in their respective countries.

In light of the fact that this was one of the earliest localized scripted dramas targeting the young generation in China, the mode of localization was not too different from the earlier strategies. A comparison of the TV format adopted between the televised text in Korea and China gives us insight into what Chinese youth could get from the TV format and what is being left out for them. As the drama features the romance between a poor girl and a wealthy boy and takes place in an elite school, the discrepancy in the plot foregrounds the kind of class relationship Chinese TV stations tolerated, and how the production coped with the "class conflict," if it had to exist on television. However, while the resulting solution of resolving the presumably tense class relationships illustrates the controlled and mediated environment of the youth audience in China, we also witness how the youth audience could make sense of the contradictory relationship, something they would have not been able to do without the adopted TV formats. In other words, the representation of the different socio-economic status of the young lovers provokes young audiences to explore their own issues – a quite new phenomenon in China.

The Chinese version is entitled *Let's Go Watch the Meteor Shower*, in which a girl Chu Yuxun, from a working-class family, enters the elite university Aliston Business College, thanks to her academic merit. It was her uncle, however, that saved money to pay the high tuition fees. Murong Yunhai, Duanmu Lei, Shangguan Ruiqian, and Ye Shuo are the rich boys and they are also the sons of the financial patrons of Aliston. Out of mischief, boredom, and youthful rebelliousness, the four boys played tricks and pranks on Chu. But finally, the four boys were moved by Chu's independence and frankness, and Murong and Chu then fell in love. In the end, the H4 (a variation of the original story's F4) found their life goals and became grown-ups with a sense of responsibility and diligence, apparently a more positive outcome than in the Korean version.

A comparison between Korean and Chinese texts reveals that the class issue is much diluted in the Chinese version (Fung and Choe 2013). The logic is simple. We can see that, in 2011, with a poverty line set at RMB 2300 (approximately US$363), 128 million Chinese were considered to be living below the poverty line. The Gini percentage, which represents the income distribution of a nation, released by the Central Intelligence Agency (CIA) was 47, close to the 45 of the United States, but high when compared to Japan (38), The Netherlands (25) or the UK (32) (CIA 2016). In this so-called socialist state, in which "harmony" was given the top priority to avoid social turmoil, dissent, and protest (Fung 2010), the state-owned media must try their utmost to suppress the social sensibility about the deteriorating social inequality. In the Chinese version, because of Chu Yuxun's outstanding performance, her uncle is willing to pay the tuition fees for her schooling. In the TV drama then, the scarcity of resources is being compensated by other factors and, therefore, bottom-up resistance from the working class is played down.

In the Chinese version of *Meteor Garden*, the rich mother of the leader of H4, Murong Yunhai, was typically portrayed as a more "reasonable" tycoon. Her hostility or even her bias against the working class as portrayed in the Korean version is toned down in the Chinese drama. First of all, she is seen as an awe-inspiring person. She respects the dignity of her subordinates while she is very strict to her own son and daughters in family education. In contrast, the same character in the Korean version is portrayed as an indifferent and unsympathetic person. She simply shows no feelings; rarely can we see any obvious emotional expressions on her face. With total control over both her business and family, the mother in the Korean version is called by others "the old witch, devil." However, in the Chinese version, no such pejorative labeling is given to the "mum." It should be noted that a major technique used in both dramas to dilute or aggravate the conflict is by means of labeling. Yet, such labeling in the Chinese version is created in a way that few labels imply social status differences.

While the poverty of the working class is covered up, the greediness of the nouveaux riches in China is downplayed. In the Chinese version, the familial setting of the main actress Chu Yuxun's family is constructed very differently. Chu lives with her mother and mother's younger brother. Chu's mother is conceived as an honest, humble, and hard-working traditional Chinese mother who has very simple expectations for her daughter's life. Whenever Chu feels big pressure from the elite school, she would say, "Just drop it if you feel exhausted" (Ep8). When the rumor about Chu and Murong's date was spread, this conventional mother blamed Chu, "Why didn't you cherish yourself? I never expect you to marry a rich guy. Just wish you well with your study and be a reliable person" (Ep12). On the contrary, her uncle has an intense desire that Chu could marry a rich guy from the upper class, but not as much as in the Korean version. Chu's mother was plotted to have direct conflicts with Shen, Murong's mother. When Chu's new tea-shop opened, Shen came to insult them and allegedly asserted that the shop received financial support from her son. Chu's mother reacted, "Then we will close it down [if it is Murong's money]!" (Ep22).

In the end, the invisibility of inequality is evinced by the presence and absence of the conflicts between the upper and working class. In the Chinese version, we could hardly locate any figure that clearly represents the interests of the working class – not even the female protagonist Chu. Thus, the love of young kids is framed as the imaginary notion that dissolves the boundaries between the rich and the poor. What we want to emphasize is that love does not work directly; it has to work through cultural capital, which involves some kind of "exchange" between the upper class and the working class in the process (Bourdieu 2010: 227). A prerequisite of a successful relationship means that the working class (Chu in the Chinese version) is required to accumulate cultural capital through educational qualifications in an elite college. The narrative of the drama implies that the outstanding performance of Chu and her ambition are good qualities to match up with Murong's family. For instance, Murong's father thought Chu would help his son with his studies and lead him to work hard, so he strongly supported their relationship. Episode 22 describes how, when their relationship takes more concrete shape, the very positive consequence is that Chu helps Murong with homework and studies. In other words, love does not abolish the class system of the society, but when the young lovers are in a romantic relationship, the relationship might compel the working class to attain a certain level of cultural capital that corresponds with members of the upper class.

In sum, in such a period (before 2010), rewriting of the plot and the twisting of the narratives, the localized TV format *Meteor Garden* remains the state's ideological machine that targets the young generation. At this juncture, it seems that the state was quite successful to manage imported culture to produce popular culture for youth that fits the ideological agenda of the state. The class issue, for instance in the adaptation of *Meteor Garden*, is contained. In other words, a one-sided or sanitized message is produced that may allow less space for alternative readings. It is also difficult to gauge whether Chinese youth would be sensitized by this highly modified content. Yet, the idol dramas did start a new epoch in which youth are overt targets of co-optation. Ironically, when the state addresses youth and young idols, the state has to unveil the mask of the latter: The material desires of the youth, their liberal views toward family and work, aesthetics – without politics though – have to be addressed and synchronized in the cultural content produced and cloned.

RUNNING MAN: THE TURN TO GAMIFICATION

So far, what we have demonstrated is the development in which localization of global and regional TV formats is highly monitored by the authorities, and the more the cultural localization, the more impotent the state apparatus is. This development is quite opposite to the increasingly greater variety of East Asian youngster culture and a pluralism of cultural content. Nevertheless, an important change took place after 2010 with the cloning of regional TV formats in China, in particular, reality TV, which is less geared to the state agenda. One determining factor is that the TV formats localized during this stage of China's cultural globalization are predominantly Korean game shows.

Without dwelling in depth on the impact of the Hallyu or Korean wave (see Chua 2004, 2012), it is not an exaggeration to say that Korean popular culture is prevalent in China after 2010, particularly reality game shows. Once these TV programs are produced and broadcast in Korea, Chinese fans would upload them and one could readily find them on legal or illegal sites. Among them, *Running Man* produced by Seoul Broadcasting System (SBS) Corporation and *Where Are We Going, Dad?* produced by Munhwa Broadcasting Corporation, both celebrity reality TV programs, were immensely popular in 2010 and 2013 respectively.

In the light of the nature of these reality TV game shows, which consist primarily of unscripted gaming among Chinese celebrities, there is little room for the station, hence the state, to dictate, twist, and prescribe the resultant contents. Unlike the scripted TV drama formatted earlier that allowed for meticulous fine-tuning to cater to the interests of the state, the acting of celebrities in the game shows is mostly ad hoc and unplanned. While Chinese audiences are enchanted by this more "natural" and uncensored entertainment, there is also no easy rationale for the state to ban or censor game shows – mostly athletic games or hide-and-seek in kind – which are, apparently, apolitical.

Running Man is a reality game show in which the hosts of the program and invited artists formed two camps to compete for the championship by playing games and finishing tasks in different locations in Korea. While this format may arguably be appealing to a general audience, the localized program reaches primarily a youth audience for two reasons. First, many famous young idols, including Angelababy and Xiaoming Huang, take part. Second, Korean versions of *Running Man* are already well-read by young netizens, generating discourses and interest among the young audience. As a strategy of the program, Zhejiang Satellite Television also posted public ads to recruit "youth volunteers" to interact with the celebrities when the show was shot at different locations.

In 2014, Zhejiang Satellite Television of China co-produced with SBS the Chinese version of *Running Man*, or in Chinese, *Hurry Up, Brother*. Such localization would not be a surprise to Chinese audiences at all, as reality format adoption in China is growing at a rapid rate. In 2015, it was reported that there are around 200 reality programs released in just one year and many are cloned formats (Zhang 2014).

The intriguing question is how the localization takes place and how it helps shape youth culture.[1] What is relevant to our argument is the specific changes made to the Chinese version of *Running Man*. In the original version, it was a game show that happens in a wide range of places from indoor to outdoor sites. The localization of *Running Man* actually unconsciously created a Chinese indoor, cardboard cosmopolitanism given that most games take place in an indoor setting, thus de-contextualizing the program from the actual setting of the Chinese community. Where around one-third of the games of the original Korean *Running Man* happen outdoors (Lau 2016), in the Chinese version the game show was usually produced at an indoor site. Among the 30 episodes in a single season, only two episodes were made in real rural areas or villages, while others were made in artificially made film sets. In a specific episode (season 2, episode 1) where a game about

---

[1] The data and analysis of the Chinese version of *Running Man*, and its comparison to the original version, are provided by, and with the permission of, Jenny Lau who has done a comprehensive comparison of these two versions.

farming was produced, an artificial farmstead was constructed to simulate the rural in a studio that was located in a city area surrounded by high-rise flats and busy traffic. A panoramic shot was deliberately taken to give the audience a sense of the modernized city – implying that under the forces of modernization, the rural is gone, not just forgotten, so it has to be re-built.

Because the games are usually produced in artificial venues, there is rarely interaction between the artists and ordinary people. In the three seasons of the Chinese *Running Man*, only five episodes feature such interaction, accounting for 16.7 percent of total episodes. Even in a setting in a convenience store, which is commonly seen in urban areas (season 3, episode 3), a mock store was fabricated. We paid visits to Zhejiang Television and chatted with television producers in October 2011. Although the localization of *Running Man* was made after our visit, the general answer we perceived is that the TV station tends to produce entertainment programs that are apolitical in nature with the intention to avoid political risks. Thus, for *Running Man*, the decontextualized production can be seen as a consistent strategy for the station to evade politics. Yet, when season 3 of *Running Man* became hotly debated in public discourse all over China at the end of 2015, the State Administration of Press, Publication, Radio, Film and Television (SARFT) had no choice but to issue a warning requiring all reality shows to improve the participation of ordinary people (Li 2015). Possibly the Chinese state was made aware of the excessive amount of advertisements in the reality shows and it felt compelled to re-direct the over-commercialized program back to one that is more connected to society. *Running Man*, nevertheless, remains a decontextualized and sanitized program that is cleared of any potential political risks.

Paradoxically, this process of localization of the reality show produces a gamification of reality in which youth idols and fans are immersed in pleasure in an urban setting, disconnected and devoid of any social problems related to rurality, unequal social development, and policy implementation. The localization, as we want to argue, indirectly produces a surreal image that China enters an epoch of modernity where problems of backwardness and other problems such as poverty and social inequality no longer exist. On the one hand, the production aligns with the state interest which always advocates the discourse of harmony (Fung 2010). On the other hand, from the perspective of the youth audience, the television game show is a kind of television program stripped of any political overtones and ideological propaganda of the state, different from the official, dogmatic, domestic TV programs they are used to. Again, this is because the game show is portrayed largely as a form of pure entertainment or gamification, suddenly giving young audiences the chance to express their pleasure in daily discourse or online forums. Should today's PRC be vigilant of cultural globalization, the values of which might lead to any political deviance, then youth's discourse on the gamified reality of *Running Man* would be an exceptional cultural space that the state would not care about. By the very nature of the game show or the entertaining nature of a Korean reality show, it is by default in the eyes of the state apolitical. Then for the fans who discuss this localized Korean show – probably together with fans who are exposed to various K-pop, Korean dramas and movies online that made pirated copies available – they derive pleasure and develop fantasies from the media content of the game show which prioritize emotions over information and play over practices. This resonates with the argument of play theory (Stephenson 1988): it is inside the free play or casual discussion of Korean popular culture that they might occasionally ponder the changes of their own Chinese society. This new cultural space of discussion would not have happened without the artificial affixing of a Korean format to the Chinese TV program. Following *Running Man*, similar cloned Korean game shows, especially *Where Are We Going, Dad?*, enhance the effect of gamification. We expect that as these sanitized localized programs seem innocuous to the Chinese state, more of these Korean or regionally adopted reality shows will appear in China in the years to come.

POPULAR MUSIC AND FANDOM

Other than reality TV shows, popular music from overseas, including Chinese-speaking regions such as Hong Kong and Taiwan, and other Asian countries, are part of a regional culture that plays a major role in shaping youth culture in China, as we have also seen in chapter 2. When compared to television, popular music seems to be a stronger force for youth culture formation as fans form themselves into communities, whether online or offline. The possibility that these fans may organize and mobilize for their beliefs and values is a matter of concern for the state. Occasionally, the state has indeed been disturbed and taken repressive measures, as we have already shown when discussing the bans on music festivals.

Chinese fans get to know their idols mostly or initially through the Internet nowadays. As media reports on music stars do not usually mingle with politics in China, control over them is comparatively less stringent. Media – in particular the Internet – have become an important channel for crystallization of fandom. Thus, the greatest threat to the state is not the reporting of idols per se, but the mobilization of youth as fans into online and offline collectivities. Such mobilization is particularly effective and affective with popular artists because their music is not just about melody, rhythm, beat, harmony, and lyrics – all these elements are embedded within a set of semiotics of meaning that can engender a sense of community and crystallize imaginary identities for audiences (McClary and Walser 1990). The resulting fandom then opens up a plurality of meaning and space for youth. While such fandom is usually frowned or looked down upon by parents and adults as foolish, trivial, naïve, and meaningless, youngsters themselves take their fandom seriously and retrieve from their communities scripts of reality and moments of strong identification.

Seen in this light, it is hardly surprising that earlier forms of fandom were much contained and steered by the state by means of censorship and co-optation. Similar to earlier globalization of TV formats that stabilizes the status quo, the import of the Taiwanese music of Jay Chou at the beginning of the new millennium, for instance, prescribes how a young Chinese should behave. In terms of image, Jay Chou is able to combine his cool looks with R&B and other "Western" musical forms as well as Chinese melodic styles, themes, and rhythms to manufacture a sort of Chineseness, as demonstrated successfully in his hits "Dong Feng Po" (2003) and "Shuang Jie Gun" (2001). There, Chinese musical genres and Chinese martial arts are mobilized and epitomized as a symbol of Chineseness (Fung 2008a). Ideologically, individualism is often encouraged, as suggested in his song "Snail" (2001), basically a self-narration of his own successful story, where an individual youth should climb up slowly and patiently as a snail on the social ladder, rather than carrying on a revolution, a story reminiscent of that of the poor girl in the Taiwanese TV drama *Meteor Garden*. That Jay Chou's works are listed as one of the "educational" materials for high school students in Shanghai was a public gesture by the government to embrace this non-confrontational and safe youth culture into the formal Chinese culture.

Then in 2005, Li Yuchun pushed more at the boundaries of the permissible. Li Yuchun was the winner of the singing contest *Super Girl* or *Super Female Voice* in summer 2005, organized by Hunan Satellite Television, the same station that aired the previously analyzed *Let's Go Watch the Meteor Shower*. *Super Girl* was a mix of the proven televised formats of ITV's *Pop Idol* (UK) and *American Idol* (Fox Network USA) and the interactive audience participation of the format of BBC's *Fame Academy*, in which ordinary people can vote via short instant messages (SMS) to pick the candidate they like. This is equivalent to giving everyone the right to vote, triggering the imagination of citizens and alluding to the potential democratic implications of the show (Fung 2013b). Li Yuchun, in that sense, can be regarded as the resulting icon of a universal referendum, democracy, or deliberation in China (Meng 2009). From our point of view, this claim is dubious. Or, in the words of Meng, "[A]s long as institutionalized channels for civic engagement and political participation remain tightly controlled in China, the rather misplaced enthusiasm on the democratic implications of *Super Girl* is an indication of how far China is from democracy rather than of how close it has come to it" (2009: 269).

With the incidental formation of deliberative fandom during the course of the show, the state tightened its control and banned any public voting for contestants. The producer of *Super Girl* explained to us in an interview in March 2016 that popular voting indeed became a contentious issue, and the authorities did not allow it anymore. The state also starts to be cautious about the consequences of the import of global culture in which fans' appropriation of not only the music or music style, but of the persona might have further consequences and implications. As fans might still form a far-distant fandom around global singers or celebrities that is hazardous to the state, in March 2016 the PRC formally banned all foreign import of online content. Thus, the latest formation of fandom is confined to the domestic realm in China, where the performance and stardom formation would be more safely cleansed of political dangers.

In this chapter, however, we want to draw attention to another, new kind of fandom that has gradually taken shape in China concomitantly: one that is apparently non-political, non-mainstream (in the sense that it is not created by major stations), and non-ideological. Such fandom – probably one of the even younger or primary school-children – comes not from individual singers, but from two different musical groups: SNH48 and TFboys. Both are derivatives of their Japanese and Korean equivalents. Both provide a cultural space for youth to create a new discourse that has not been seen in China before or even does not intersect with any of the existing domains of Chinese culture. Youth discourse retreats quite ironically from the pursuit of individualism to collective cuteness, from looking for deliberation to alternatives, and from Chineseness to non-Chineseness. The implication for the development of youth culture is of vital importance.

THE CHINESE AKB48: IRRELEVANCE TO POLITICS

SNH48, based in Shanghai, are a sister Chinese idol group of the Japanese AKB48, who are arguably the most popular girl band in Japan at this moment, and one of the most successful girl group exports to other areas in Asia. In 2012, Chinese company Ninestyle collaborated with the management company of AKB48, AKS Company, to set up the first Chinese girl group SNH48. While girl idols are not new in China, SNH48 are distinct in their model of replicating AKB48 to sell, and, more importantly, in their formula of selling, "the idols you can meet," that resonates with today's global youth culture's characteristics of interactivity, immediate care, and direct communication.

The "foreignness" of SNH48 was evident. In the first place, they perform the Chinese dubbed version of AKB48's original songs, including the "Halloween Night," "Ponytail to Shushu," and "Take Me Five," to name a few. Even the arrangement of the songs are not different from the Japanese versions. When the lyrics are translated, the contents remain the same. In these three abovementioned music videos, SNH48 basically modeled the plot, acting, and costume of AKB48 on the original videos. For instance, in SNH48's "Take Me Five," except for a short episode of a few members of SNH48 listening to an old man, the video featured the members playing musical instruments while singing and wearing similar boyish and black outfits. Interestingly, it is this ostensible importation and mimicry of Japanese culture, perceived to be so distinct from the mainstream Chinese youth culture, that makes SNH48 a rather safe icon of marginality in the eyes of the authorities. On the one hand, in our informal talks with personnel at Sina Music and Universal Music in Beijing in February 2016, no one attaches any importance to SNH48; they are usually regarded as young fetish symbols outside the domain of Chinese culture. On the other hand, they seem to have succeeded in establishing a strong fan base. In Wechat, one popular member Yitong Li has 720,000 followers (as of March 2016). And in the same year as their debut, the group could hold a concert in Guangzhou with an audience of 10,000, comparable to many established singers in China.

The most astonishing scene is the video for "Ponytail to Shushu," which displays the bubbling gaiety of SNH48 on a beach with white sand and blue ocean, and, more unconventionally, with the girls wearing bikinis while dancing. Such a scene with female teenagers wearing swimsuits is rarely seen on any mass media in China. However, it seems that SNH48 do not upset any audience or authority in China, or at least, there is no conservative criticism heard in any formal channel about their potential sexy openness. The reason is obvious. In the eyes of the Chinese authorities, SNH48 are just one of the girlish subcultures: they are trivial, unchallenging to the status quo, and above all, they have nothing to do with politics and are culturally very distant from China. Compared to *Super Girl*, whose mechanism of voting on TV was finally banned by SARFT, SNH48's cultural distance and appearance of triviality keep their public election safely in place, where the voting can be publicly discussed and promoted, and it is organized in the centrally located Shanghai Mercedes Benz Cultural Centre. On SNH48's official website, the election outcome was festively announced, highlighting the winner's score of more than 70,000 votes. We would argue that it is the group's apoliticalness and irrelevance that offer them a space, at least temporarily, outside surveillance, in which youth could interact and engage with each other, utter and pronounce their views, and discharge their emotion and energy.

In terms of media exposure, SNH48 remain largely non-mainstream, at least, during their first and second year of formation. Members of SNH48 acted in short films that broadcast largely on online channels (e.g. *Soulvenir* in 2016) or in low budget films shown in cinemas (e.g. *Balala the Fairies: Princess Camellia* in 2015). Members also acted in online dramas in Sohu, Youku, Tudou, and Mango TV online. Some members also performed in theater plays, which is a more alternative cultural form in China. Their non-mainstream strategies successfully position and reposition themselves as just girls, teenagers, marginal, and alternative. All these strategies show that it is not so much the state that stops them from going mainstream; it is their own positioning which eventually gives more room for youth and group members to maneuver.

Based on media reports and our own observations on the original AKB48 performance in their live house in Akihabara in February 2016, most of the fans were male and during the performance, there was a high intensity of interaction between AKB48 members on stage and the floor; fans quickly responded to the performance with laughter, gestures, and yelling from their own seats. The same model was mimicked in China with SNH48 always engaging their fans during live performances, with the only difference being a roughly even distribution of male and female fans. Like AKB48, their engagements with the fans constitute an ongoing process in the form of seasonal concerts, yearly award and singing tour, theater performance and the "election." The last of these is worth discussing in greater detail. It is a very complicated system in which members of the group are elected to take the lead. The entire system of recruitment and promotion is fairly in line with the normal bureaucratic system of formal and other arts education in China, that is, anyone who aspires to be a singer can go for an audition, and when members are enrolled in the group, they need to excel.

In SNH48, there are five teams with each team having their own team leader to be elected (depending on popularity), and the first batch of singers to be lined up for the next single. Currently with 115 members in the whole group, they feed into an essentially multi-vocal star image, whereby audiences can attach to any of these girls their different hopes and aspirations. In short, this election system replicates the kind of schooling and examination system in Chinese youth's everyday life. At the same time, it presents a somewhat better system in which even the most ordinary girls can compete and win, without much of the predisposed social economic capital or *guanxi* necessary in the official education culture. Their open discussion and transparency online in various social media and websites, from QQ to *Baidu*, demonstrate a form of open participation, if not democratic participation.

In line with most fandom studies, the creative space created is not only limited to the cultural form of SNH48; fans' direct rendezvous with members of SNH48 offers another level of space where youth could experience and express themselves. These fans' direct engagement and their perceived synchronization with the culture of SNH48 itself is the new space never understood by the authorities who might think that the space is trivial, irrelevant, and unthreatening. But to the youth, it is the place where they enjoy their autonomy, narrate their own discourse, and make sense of their own language and gesture.

The cultural synchronization between members and fans creates something unconventional. The relationship between members and fans is not so much on the level of appropriation of cultural practices, values, persona, or images, as we discussed regarding cultural globalization in chapter 2. Singers in SNH48 are ordinary cute girls and so are the fans. Like AKB48, the essence of SNH48 and fandom is not so much about politics, and even not about the politics of culture, but rather cuteness or *kawaii* in Japanese. Unlike the *Super Girl* idol Li

Yuchun, whom some publics turned into an icon for the lesbian community, the female image of SNH48 is never controversial. The girls represent a more feminine image or even a super-girlish image – always dressing up in pink, blue, or checked uniform with laced mini-skirt or in swimming suit – that is more stereotypical than any of the Chinese female images. As for the music style and content, it tells the everyday life of teenage girls. From their first EP *Heavy Rotation* in 2013 to their tenth EP *New Year's Bell* in 2015, the songs are mainly romantic or poppy love songs that talk about feelings of love, promises, and dates in different seasons, climates, festivals, Halloween night, and New Year.

Then it comes to the final question of localization. If the image, operation, and fandom of SNH48 is in essence so Japanese, what does it actually mean? While chapter 2 illustrates a period of cultural globalization in China, here Chinese youth, in particular the very young, seem to pursue much less filtered regional cultural contents as well as less deliberately localized-regionalized images. They do so as if they are aware, intuitively or not, that localization means censorship, power, and control. Thus, it is not coincidental that there is hardly any trace of Chineseness embedded in the girl group or in their cultural products. Except for the language – Putonghua – they use, SNH48's dancing style, appearance, *kawaii* look, beach photos and so forth are no different from their Japanese counterparts. The conflation goes even further when concurrent members of AKB48 Mariya Suzuki and SKE48 (sister group of AKB48 in Japan) Miyazawa Sae joined SNH48 in 2013 and became leaders of their teams in October 2013, after formal approval from the Chinese government. It is true that the Sino-Japanese diplomatic relationship had been bumpy in the previous five years but such joint formation of girlish groups is the most non-harmful and non-threatening cultural engagement to the authorities. It is in this small niche that Chinese youth of the next generation find a comfortable zone to survive.

TFBOYS AND KOREAN IMAGINATION

Another similar example of this direct adoption or minimal localization of regional, inter-Asian youth culture is TFBoys – which could be viewed as the male counterpart of SNH48 – who originated, in this case, from Korean, not Japanese, pop culture. TFBoys (The Fighting Boys) are a Chinese boy band with three members: Roy, Jackson, and Karry. While Karry was born in 1999, the other two members were born in 2000, which means they are meant to target teenagers – their contemporaries – younger people. Chinese company TF Entertainment pulled together this trio in 2013 as they discovered these boys have talents in dancing and singing. It is unclear which Korean boy bands they took reference from, as top K-pop boy bands usually have between five and twelve members – except TVXQ! which had only two members (Hub 2015). Accordingly, their image is much younger than SNH48 whose members are around the age of 20. On stage, when members of TFBoys dance, they look no different from K-pop boy bands such as MBLAQ, 2PM or B2ST. As far as their public image or their image in music videos is concerned, they look like "ordinary boys" with a Korean outfit, haircut, and make-up.

The success story of TFBoys is similar to that of SNH48. In September 2011, TF Family was formed as a platform to enroll members, and candidates had to go through various "tests" to become members. Their early accomplishment was also achieved via the Internet, where Karry's song "Trapped Bird" was circulated nationwide and later Karry and Roy's duet, "One is Similar to Summer, one is Similar to Autumn" became popular on *Weibo*. Between 2013 and 2015, they released three popular Putonghua albums, *Heart* (2013), *Manuals of Youth* (2014), and *Big Dreamer* (2015), which included big hits. On *Weibo*, official fans number 4.74 million. On *Baidu Tieba*, members reached one million, while followers on QQ reached 12 million (as of March 2016).

Most of their fans are female, as seen from their performances on CCTV and Hunan Satellite TV.

By and large, the three members of TFBoys project an ordinary young, pretty boyish image with decent manner and proper attire. On screen, they usually dress in simple T-shirts. On stage they wear uniform or slim-cut suits, sometimes in black and white, sometimes in fancy colors – basically commonly recognized as Korean style. After a talk given by one of the authors in Beijing in November 2015 about Korean pop culture, he gathered together a few female university students and asked them for their perceptions of TFBoys. They were all crazy about them, but they also expressed that they were perhaps too old, confirming the much younger fan base of TFBoys. What these female university students value is the purity of the young boys, and the feeling that they are approachable. They also remarked on the similarity between the boy idols and the fans.

While this new mode of idol–fan relationship can be understood as part of a marketing strategy, it also suggests another form of communication and interaction, which is less hierarchical. In the case of TFBoys, there is no election involved and face-to-face gathering with fans is common. TF Entertainment started to organize a TF fans gathering night in Beijing's LeSports Center and Beijing Capital Sports Complex in 2015. Online, the space created for discussion is huge. Notwithstanding the rules, for example, in *Baidu Tieba*, governing what posts can be made and under what conditions they are required to be deleted, these fans rehearse and experience the possibility of free expression and discussion through their praise of and comments about TFBoys.

Without romanticizing such fan practices, we do want to contend for their potential in supplying the fundamentals on which new cultural spaces for youth can be constructed and their cultural practices normalized. This regional form of globalization demonstrates not so much the global drives for change as regional affinity and mimicry for the potential to change. Given the healthy and innocent image of the three boys, the state is rendered less alert to such potential of youth culture. At least, for the time being, they do not pose any threat to realpolitik.

CONCLUSION

In this chapter, we have illustrated the emergence of a youth space, largely constituted by regional, inter-Asian cultural flows and unnoticed by the state, which is more sensitive and cautious towards the influx of global culture. While the latter is heavily monitored and regulated, and the potential for cultural resistance minimized, the regionalization of global culture has produced something the state remains unaware of, precisely because this something does not bear the usual resemblance to politics.

We have shown how the adaptation and production of the drama series *Meteor Garden* in China is an attempt to dilute the issue of class inequality. Yet, as outlined earlier, the localization of Korean TV game shows ushers in a process of gamification of reality that is separated from any real social contexts in China. Such game shows offer Chinese producers one of the most apolitical and safe regional cultures, a convenient format to steer away from official intervention and troubles. But precisely this decontextualized, entertaining nature of the show crystallizes youth fan culture into everyday discourses, online and offline, which allow them to freely engage with each other, interact and play. Without showing any hint that they are talking about politics, in its strict and explicit sense, the very free discussion as such constitutes a cultural space that is seldom interrupted and dominated by state discourses such as the discourse of "harmony" and the "China Dream."

The replication of Japanese girl bands and Korean boy bands generates similar effects. For the Chinese authorities, the conventional strategy has always been to advance the economy by globalizing China's media landscape, that is provided that such advancement does not become hazardous to social security and thus upsetting the status quo. As long as these localized cultural products like SNH48 and TFBoys appear to be nothing more than entertainment, trivial, and unthreatening, they are left to their own devices.

At the same time, the formation of such new forms of fandom deserves our attention because it is different from earlier engagements between fans and idols. Idols of previous generations, such as Jay Chou and Li Yuchun, provide cultural and star texts of Chineseness and/or nationalistic sentiments that may inspire their young fans and work, intentionally or not, in tandem with the state's management of culture. But now, such inter-Asian cultural flows, whether from Japan or Korea, function most remarkably in their leveling or synchronization between fans and idols, hence the conspicuous absence of any clear learning trajectory for the young people.

Then youth in China no longer need to fight for more space for cultural maneuvering because the entertainment or the boyish and girlish cultures are the unmonitored cultural areas for the state. The state neither acts on, nor wants to monitor, the already marginal subculture. They do not even have the interest to tap into and pacify or neutralize these multifarious but trivial youth cultures. Then in this relatively autonomous space, youth, through their fandom, crystallize around the bands they like, discuss the content of popular culture freely, and feel accustomed to openly support their idols. It is not about politics apparently. In the long term, what is not certain is that, when youth grow up, and become part of the establishment, no one knows whether their habits, attitudes, and customs will give a crucial twist to various political processes.

One important note we want to insert in this chapter is that we must resist the temptation to merely frame Chinese youth practices with perspectives of consumption culture and materialistic desires. We need to go beyond and probe into spaces opened up by cultural flows, particularly, as we have shown, by regional, inter-Asian ones, spaces that operate largely outside the auspices and intervention of the Party, family, work, and education. The logic of play and the plurality of cultural practices among young Chinese incubated under the invisibility of new emergent spaces is a political act in its own right, when we consider the intrinsic value of youthfulness and the strategy to preserve it, to enjoy it the same ways as other youth populations in the region, in the world. We are also curious as to their further political potential when new cultural spaces afford Chinese youth a sense of freedom to talk, interact, and be themselves. At present, such spaces and practices develop primarily online, which may mutate and permeate other existing institutions, media productions, and digital technologies. When the state will notice and start to interrupt the formation of such youth culture, no one knows. When no one knows, any future is thinkable.

4

Chinese Heteronormativity and its Discontents

The young generation devotes itself by entering the vast stream of new social activism and movements; now is a hard time for them. A new strategy and method will be needed in the current political situation.

Wei Tingting (2015: 324)

INTRODUCTION

When strolling through the parks of Beijing at night – and only at night – we observed many young couples holding hands or kissing each other. The relative scarcity of private space inside the family and other city areas drives young lovers outdoors, in search for what we like to call public privacy. But in our current times, the park is often replaced by dating apps, many young people are now swiping away, or accepting, potential partners on Momo, gay men use Blued, ZANK, or Aloha to find someone, whereas their lesbian peers will install LesPark on their mobile phone. Online gay drama series like *Addiction* not only attract gay audiences, but also a large audience of young female fans – disturbing the authorities to the extent that they banned the show, as we will discuss in this chapter. The theme song of the show nevertheless went viral on *Weibo*. At the same time, *Weixin* groups share the latest information on issues pertaining to gender, love, and sexuality.

The openness suggested by these practices is questioned by feminist activist Wei Tingting. In her view, under the leadership of Xi Jinping,

China is facing "a 'down' time," in which they "still need to keep a low profile in the current days to see what will happen" (Wei 2015: 324). In March 2015, the authorities detained her and four other feminist activists in different parts of the country who planned a public awareness campaign against sexual harassment on public transportation. Wei Tingting, aged 27, was earlier involved in producing the *Vagina Monologues* in Wuhan. While the activists were released after a month, the detention shows how issues related to gender and sexuality remain vastly contentious in China.

Concerns over sexuality are frequently, both inside and outside China, projected upon young people. But with the opening up of China since 1978, much has changed, also in the domain of love, gender, and sexuality. This chapter engages with contemporary modes of masculinity, femininity, with love and dating cultures, and with sexuality and queer (*ku'er*) cultures in China. We will show how all these domains, that we read through the Foucauldian lens of governmentality, negotiate specific local histories with more globalized imaginaries. We will do so in five steps. We will first engage with the discourse of heteronormativity and its specific articulations in China. After this, we will analyze studies on youth, gender, and sexuality in China, connecting these to different media representations and cultural practices like the wedding market in Shanghai. These manifestations of heteronormative discourse are not uncontested, and in the subsequent sections we focus on three different domains that negotiate heteronormativity. First, we elucidate how highly popular romance comedies in China paradoxically also poke fun at love, taking one movie – *Love Is Not Blind* (*shilian 33 tian*) – as a case in point. Second, the proliferation of queer cultures in China do challenge heteronormative norms, while at times – such as in marriages of convenience – they may also accommodate, if not validate, it. Third, and finally, sex and feminism at times challenge prevailing gender and sex roles.

While all these unsettling discourses – in romance comedy, queer culture, and in sex and feminism – hold the promise of changing paradigms related to gender and sexuality, we are quite wary of embracing them as emancipatory alternatives. We argue that a positive teleological narrative of modernization, opening up, emancipation, or liberation is far too simplistic in that it flattens contradictions and complexities of youth whose gender orientation, sexual behaviors, and masculine/feminine self-representations are constantly evolving. Inequality continues to haunt gender and sex roles in China. For example, being single is constructed, on the institutional level, as a transitional status not acceptable by the family as we illustrated in chapter 1, and on an individual level, more as a burden for women than for men, just as queer cultures are privileging young urbanites with a reasonable income. As such, the leading themes that run through this book – in connection to the role of parents, state, and school, to the role of media, both online and offline, and related processes of globalization and localization, commodification and consumption cultures, and the emergence of new young subjectivities that are both under scrutiny yet also allow for experimentation – come together in this chapter.

CHINESE GENDERS?

Under the banner of communism, Mao Zedong famously asserted that women hold up half of the sky. The focus on the people and the worker would result, so it was claimed, in more gender equality. However, it seems that it produced merely a defeminization, and thus a validation of masculinity, rather than equality (Gao and Li 2011). After 1949, the image of the worker was presented as a masculine female role model: a girl with short hair and green cap in Red Guard uniform. The modern People's Liberation Army (PLA) is still the same: women with short hair but dressed with different colors of uniform and occasionally wearing skirts; and they are "powered up" by wearing ties and given a gun. The Marriage Law passed by the PRC in the 1950s secured the free choice of a marriage partner, representing a radical change from the previous patriarchal marriage rituals and traditions, even though "familial, community, and institutional restrictions on mixed-sex interaction limited courtship in practice for much of the Maoist era" (Farrer 2002: 13). Further reform in the Second Marriage Law in 1980, apart from introducing the one child policy, legalized divorce, and further updates in 1983 allowed interracial marriage. This reflects the standard of the new generation who regard love, affection, and perhaps sexual enjoyment, as the modern criteria for marriage. Further amendment in 2003 outlawed married persons' cohabitation with a third party. This was a deliberate attempt by the state to curtail the influence of "Western-style sexual liberation" that drove the reoccurrence of concubinage in cities, as was common before 1949 (Wen 2010).

As always, the reform of the Marriage Law implicitly is aimed to tackle issues of gender and sexuality in big cities. As Harriet Evans shows, sexuality remained a significant topic, she writes (2008: 266), "throughout the Mao years, and beyond into the 1990s, sex education and medical pamphlets, articles in the women's and youth press, and Women's Federation pronouncements contributed to a dominant discourse of sexuality in which the female subject was defined largely through reproductive concerns." The 1990s and beyond have witnessed a proliferation of possible gender and sexuality roles, inspiring James Farrer to title his book on youth sex culture in Shanghai *Opening Up* (2002), and Katrien Jacobs to refer in her book's title *People's Pornography* to "a sexual rebellion within China's netizen culture" (2012: 183; see also Jacobs 2015).

But does an increased visibility signal an increased freedom? After all, as Foucault once asserted, "visibility is a trap" (1978: 200). Harriet Evans articulates a similar warning when she writes that "the contemporary production of the sexualized body – in narrative, visual, spatial and physical form – can also be read in rather different ways. Sex and its representations can work both to reaffirm and subvert the legitimacy of normative gender practices and expectations. A greater tolerance of diverse sexual practices is not, in itself, synonymous with a diversification of ideas about gender difference" (p. 363; see also Brownell and Wasserstrom's 2002 edited volume, and in particular the introductory chapter by both editors).

How, then, to analyze this tension between increased visibility and diversity and emancipation? The latter terms smack of a developmental discourse in which the self ought to be liberated from its inhibitions and repressions. In the social sciences, sex generally refers to reproductive autonomy, whereas gender refers to the roles attributed to anatomical sex (de Kloet 2008: 200). The latter definition has opened up a discourse on the possibility of performing and molding one's gender, ranging from Simone de Beauvoir's assertion that one is not born a woman, to Judith Butler's work on gender performances. According to Butler, heterosexuality is crucial in the production of gender, producing a heteronormative discourse that seeps through everyday life in all its details (1990, 1993). In this discourse, one's anatomical sex defines one's gender, which in turn produces a heterosexual desire. Not only does a gay subjectivity undermine such a chain of equivalences; other forms of gender performances, such as transgenderism, also help unsettle the heterosexual matrix.

One example from China helps to illustrate the complexity. In 2010, a Chinese boy named Liu Zhu from the Sichuan Conservatory of Music joined the *Super Boy* competition on Hunan Television. Wearing high heels, stockings, and with long hair, he performed on the TV show and unsettled the jury, who questioned if he really was a boy and even requested he present ID to attest his sex category. The rude interrogation of the jury caused quite some debate on the Chinese Internet, and Liu Zhu actually made it to the next round, where he was finally eliminated. His performance upsets conventional causalities that exist between sex and gender, and his transgender performance was not articulated along lines of homosexuality; according to him, this is simply the way he prefers to dress. (For a discussion of the related phenomenon of *weiniang* (literally fake women, or the cosplay (from costume play, where participants dress to represent a particular character) practices of boys dressed up as girls), see Chow forthcoming.) Some years earlier, in the female version of the TV contest *Super Girl*, winner Li Yuchun also revealed gender performances that challenged norms of how a Chinese girl should look, and with her boyish looks, she quickly became the icon of the gay and lesbian communities in China, as we have already discussed in chapter 3.

Such quite spectacular gender performances can, however, also be read as pointing to the increasingly abundant proliferation of discourses around sexuality. This was Foucault's argument in his *History of Sexuality*. His repression hypothesis postulates that it is exactly the claim of repression that allowed for an abundant proliferation of discourses about sexuality; in his words, "What is peculiar to modern societies, in fact, is not that they consigned sex to a shadow existence, but that they dedicated themselves to speaking of it *ad infinitum*, while exploiting it as *the* secret" (Foucault 1978: 35). Sexuality, and in its slipstream the body, was over the course of the nineteenth century in the West turned into a site of biopower; it was constructed as the site where one could speak the truth of oneself. But, as Foucault warns elsewhere, "maybe the target nowadays is not to discover what we are but to refuse what we are....We have to promote new forms of subjectivity through the refusal of this kind of individuality that has been imposed on us for several centuries" (Foucault 2000: 336).

These philosophical musings help us to become more skeptical about narratives of emancipation, modernization, and individualization, and their complex entanglements with gender and sexuality. The return of neo-Confucianism in China, and its support of patriarchy and hierarchy, the one child policy, the *gaokao* or public exam system, as well as the force of consumerism all constitute additional disciplinary discourses that regulate both sexuality and gender. Governmental logics constitute the relationships between wo/men and love, gender and sexuality, they produce the conditions of possibility to love and to be loved, to express or hide one's gender and to explore or (try to) ignore one's sexual desire (Foucault et al. 2007: 96).

While heteronormativity is anything but uniquely Chinese, in China, it gets its specific articulations, in which in particular neo-Confucian discourses and the one child policy play an important role, as we have shown in chapter 1. In this chapter we would like to probe into practices that may unsettle these heteronormative discourses, but following the main thrust of this book, and also our hesitation to embrace the narrative of visibility and emancipation, we acknowledge that such unsettling necessarily will also entail new modes of governmentality, new forms of control, and may even help to strengthen that which it seems to oppose. But let us start by exploring some articulations of discourses of heteronormativity that are part and parcel of the governmental logics of the state, the school, and the family.

HETERONORMATIVE ASPIRATIONS I: SURVEY FINDINGS

Our exploration into the articulations of heteronormative discourse in China starts at a rather unlikely place: numbers and statistics. These figures not only give us some insight into recent opinions and attitudes, but also allow us to read them at a meta-level, namely as an articulation of a discourse on "healthy sexuality" and "proper gender roles."

Studies on sexuality in China, for instance, focus on the age people marry, thereby consolidating the importance attached to the idea of getting married. They show how the age for marriage is moving upward, for males from 23.6 in 1990 to 25.9 in 2010 and for females from 22 to 23.9 (Lu and Wang 2013: 64). In the city, the age increased from 23.6 to 26, whereas in the countryside people marry younger, there the age increased from 22.5 to 23.7 (Lu and Wang 2013: 64). The average age that people start having sex is, as expected, much lower. A report called *2015 Marriage Report of Chinese People* released by the Institute of Social Science Survey from Peking University reveals that the first-time-sex age of Chinese people has declined. For instance, according to this report, the average age for first-time sex among those born after 1995, 1990, 1985, and 1980 is 17.7, 19.8, 21.3, and 22.1, respectively, while for people born before 1980 this is 22.7 (Beijing News 2016). Chinese youth thus have earlier sex than before, but they marry later, especially in urban areas. These findings suggest that they experiment more with love and sexuality than before. An online study among 163 young Chinese from the post-1980s generation confirms this: 55.2 percent of the girls and 45.7 percent of the boys had had sex with more than one partner (Ruan 2011: 216). Knowledge of sex is derived from multiple sources, but education does not feature prominently here. A study from 2007 among university students revealed that 67.3 percent did not receive sex education (Li 2008: 8). In two studies, books are claimed to be the most important source of knowledge related to sexuality (Li and Niu 2008: 8; Lu and Che 2009: 44). This is followed in one study by friends and schoolmates, media, school, and, lastly, family (Lu and Che 2009: 44). The other study ranks the Internet as the second most important source, followed by same-sex friends, films and series, school, and, finally, parents (Li and Niu 2008: 8). What both studies attest to is the limited importance of both school and parents when it comes to information on sex and love, and the relative importance of books, media, and friends. What all studies conclude is that better sex education is crucial for China, thereby promoting notions of "healthy sex." This is in line with Day Wong's summary of the mission of the *Chinese Journal of Human Sexuality*, published by China's Department of Health, which "highlights its three-fold mission: popularize sexual science, promote sexual health and build sexual harmony" (Wong 2015: 103).

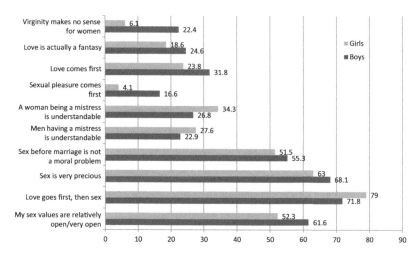

Figure 4.1. Sex values among Chinese teenagers
Source: Huang and Pan 2012: 57

A study in 2010 by Huang and Pan among 1,593 teenagers, randomly sampled all over China in 123 urban areas and 37 rural areas, and aged between 14 and 17 years, presents their values about love and sexuality (Huang and Pan 2012) (see figure 4.1). These figures tell us that while the majority claim their sex values to be relatively or very open, still almost half of the sample do not support sex before marriage. Of the same sample, a quite remarkable 71.2 percent of the boys and 76.7 percent of the girls agree that masturbation is not good. In another qualitative study, the authors quote a 23-year-old woman saying that

> I can only accept premarital sex if the two people love each other, and they are both adults, and they have the ability to tell right from wrong, and they can be responsible for their own behavior. Juveniles' sex is unacceptable. (Fan and Shen 2015: 85)

A 22-year-old man considered sex before marriage a wise choice in order to avoid disappointments during marriage (Fan and Shen 2015: 85):

> Premarital sex is very important. It happens naturally when your love goes deeper. It's really not good to hold it back. If you don't do it, you might have sex problems after marriage. It's normal to let the other person know about everything you are.

A study among the generation born in the 1990s shows that the older respondents from this generation are becoming more pragmatic in terms of marriage, compared to their younger peers; 8 percent fewer accept a "naked marriage," a term used in China for marriage based solely on love. As the authors of the study write, countering the stereotype that this is not a serious generation:

> When marriage is getting closer they become more anxious. They don't have the courage to face an unsure future. A realistic time needs a realistic love, who can say this is not a serious attitude. Comparing to hurting each other after your dream is broken down, people would rather think about their choice before they make it. (Yuan and Zhang 2011: 56, see also Jankowiak 2013)

These studies suggest that while sexual values are "opening up" alongside the opening up of the country, we need to be careful about proclaiming that a sexual revolution has taken, or is taking, place. The figures do indicate that Chinese youth experiment more before they marry, and allude to the importance of the media for sexual education. While less than one-third proclaimed in the last study that love comes first, and almost a quarter consider love to be fantasy, it is the trope of love that permeates popular culture most prominently, be it in songs, television series, books, or cinema. As we argued earlier, all the sources of information through which Chinese youth gain information (most prominently books, media, and friends), but also studies like the ones we quoted above, are part of a governmental logic in which the sexual lives and thoughts of young people are measured, weighed, and monitored.

HETERONORMATIVE ASPIRATIONS II: MEDIA REPRESENTATIONS

Moving from figures to representation, the recent surge in reality TV and dating shows in China help us to further grasp the resilience of heteronormative discourse. With the one child policy resulting in a skewed gender ratio with more boys than girls (according to a 2010 report 51.27 percent of Chinese citizens are males and 48.73 percent are females (Zhonghua Renmin Gongheguo Guojia Tongjiju 2011a, 2011b), concerns over dating are now high on the social agenda of the Chinese. This may well help explain the success of the TV dating show *If You Are the One* or *Feichengwurao*, created and broadcast nationwide by Jiangsu Satellite television since 2010. This show has caused heated debates and controversies over values and morality of love and marriage. In this format, a line-up of 24 female guests is presented with five male bachelors. The latter are introduced one at a time. Each bachelor is introduced through three video clips, as well as through interacting in the studio. The first clip gives his life background, the second explains what he wants from a woman, and in the third his friends express their opinions about him. In the course of the introduction, women who lose interest in dating the guy can turn off their lights. Lights still on after the three rounds are those interested ladies whom the man can select from. This guy can also choose to ask one that has turned her light off and beg her not to reject him. Similar to the *Super Girl* format we already discussed in chapter 3, this show testifies to the entertainment value of Chinese media productions, as CSM Media

Research showed that its audience reached 2.77 percent of Chinese viewers or 36 million as of May 2013, a figure far higher than any of its competitors (*Global Times* 2014).

We went to the actual shooting site of the station in Nanjing to observe the recording of the program. This TV show struck us as basically a modern version of the traditional matchmaking custom of Chinese society (*xiangqin*), except that it was now being transformed into a mediated entertainment spectacle with younger and more humorous "matchmakers" as the program host asked more sarcastic and taunting questions to those who volunteered themselves to publicize their private matters in relation to marriage choice. Given that the show was made in an urban context, the narrative of marriage was inflected with topics of love, sex, and money. The show started to attract negative attention from officials, who subsequently decreed that the show unfavorably disseminated "wrong values" and the State Administration of Radio, Film and Television finally intervened to stop the "vulgarity" of the reality portrayed (Yang 2010). In particular a girl, Manuo, who proclaimed to rather cry in a BMW than smile on the back of a bike caused huge controversies. Since then, *If You Are the One* was instructed to curb frequent chats on financial wealth and sex, and a third host was assigned to mainstream the conversation.

In a book devoted to the lifestyle of the generation born in the 1990s, titled *Our 90s!* (*Women jiulinghou!*), the authors compare the responses of different generations to this incident in the show. The authors quote a 49-year-old respondent saying:

> The girl is just 20 years old, according to her bad behavior she has no morality or ability and she is not beautiful, her own evaluation about herself is too high, and the anchor is protecting her. So Jiangsu TV makes a mistake here, think about it, such a bad person and you let her on TV, will this affect more than billions of young people's future? Most

of them are students but what is this girl showing us on TV? (Yuan and Zhang 2011: 57)

The response of someone born in the 1990s is strikingly different:

I really feel that Manuo's requirement is quite normal, just a BMW and a house, to be honest, crying in a BMW is a pretty low requirement, one of my friends said "Manuo's requirement is so low, me, I would fucking laugh in a Ferrari." I think Manuo has the capital for that. She has a beautiful face, a sexy body, and she is honest, her requirement is not high. You can buy a BMW with less than 300,000 yuan now. If you don't have even 300,000 yuan why should you marry a good girl? Nowadays girls are not materialistic, they are just realistic. (Yuan and Zhang 2011: 57)

The comparison is undoubtedly stretched in this research: opinions will vary widely, also among those born in the 1990s, but the schism between an older generation that stresses morality and is worried about the bad impact of media and a generation that is more understanding of the entanglement between love and money is telling for changing values over the generations.

The show opens up a space for Chinese youth to discuss issues related to love and dating. As Kong argues, it provides "a platform that this generation can use to articulate its own 'lifestyle politics' through self-representations and self-expression in a globalizing society" (2013: 130). In her study, Kong shows how *If You Are the One* engages with many socially relevant topics, including environmental issues, dating a foreigner, issues related to career choice, and so on. The show thus displays "the diversity of opinion among the post-1980s generation. In turn, these competing voices contribute to a public discourse on lifestyle choices as important aspects of identity and social responsibility" (Kong 2013: 143). But reality TV, together with the response of the government, is also deeply implicated in tactics of governmentality, as they promote specific forms of subjectivity while discouraging and disavowing others. Sun Wanning argues that while in communist China life narratives were predominantly prescribed by the state and society, nowadays the burden has shifted more toward the individual, who has to bear the feelings of uncertainty, vulnerability, and anxiety. A wide range of media formats, including dating shows, tap into these collective concerns (Sun 2014).

Added to the analysis above, the show also introduces the recently emerging category of *shengnü*, which stands for "leftover women." It is a derogatory term that is "widely used to describe an urban, professional female in her late twenties or older who is still single" (Fincher 2014: 2). It is paradoxical to observe that in a country where there is a surplus of men rather than women, anxieties over singlehood are still mapped onto the female body. On the whole, a *shengnü* is alleged to have some imperfections, either in appearance or personality, so that in these reality shows, leftover girls would be learning a lesson: they have to learn and be disciplined to become a normal attractive girl in order to be courted. The popularity of these programs shows how women, exceeding the golden time of marriage in their late 20s or early 30s, are interpellated into a general anxiety over the possibility of finding the right man for marriage. In their analysis of how *If You Are the One* portrays *shengnü*, Luo and Sun point to the role of experts. They quote Zheng Zihang, a popular romance writer, saying:

The [ideal] woman should appear a "big woman" [successful, capable, and presentable to the public] in public; at home, the woman should become a "little woman" [submissive, sweet, innocent]; during the day, the woman should act like a "white-boned demon" [a legendary character from the Chinese classical mythology *Journey to the West*, embodying the imagery of a beautiful, clever, wicked, and powerful woman, who, after all, can fight against the very powerful male Monkey King];

at night, the woman should turn into a "fox demon" [mischievous, seductive, and young] for her husband. (Luo and Sun 2014: 14)

Clearly, it is the woman who carries the burden for success, love, and supporting the man. As such, the show, they argue, reaffirms male privilege as well as hegemonic gender roles. Moving away from mediation to everyday life, we can see that there are serious material implications when one rushes into marriage in order to shed the stigma of being a *shengnü*. Leta Hong Fincher argues that "contrary to the stereotypes of single, professional women being miserable and lonely, I will show that the reality is quite the opposite: it is young women rushing into marriage too early that tend to wind up in trouble" (2014: 24). She argues that gender inequality is resurfacing in post-socialist China, and she analyzes this through the prism of the real estate market, where women are "willing to cede ownership of an enormously expensive home to their boyfriends or husbands, even when these women had contributed their entire life savings to the property purchase" (Fincher 2014: 6). The economic wealth of *shengnü* has become an important factor in the real estate boom, but mostly men profit, whereas only 30 percent of property includes the women's name, they do contribute in 70 percent of house purchases (2014: 18–19). For Fincher, then, *shengnü* "are a category of women concocted by the government to achieve its demographic goals of promoting marriage, planned population, and maintaining social stability" (2014: 17).

The unequally shared burden of home ownership is the theme of the television drama series *Woju* (dwelling narrowness), broadcast during the summer and autumn of 2009, adapted from a novel by Internet writer Liu Liu (Zurndorfer 2016). The story revolves around two sisters, the older of whom wants to stay in the city of Shanghai instead of returning to her hometown with her boyfriend. The young couple aims to buy an apartment, but due to their average income and the staggering house prices, this turns out to be impossible. Then the other sister comes to help. She is the mistress of the mayor's secretary, and receives all kinds of expensive gifts from him, including an apartment. This, according to the older sister, is a true declaration of love, as she proclaims:

> If a man is in love…the one thing he should offer his woman is neither his heart nor his body. He should supply his woman first with…a pile of bank notes and then a piece of property. (Zurndorfer 2016: 4)

As Zurndorfer writes, the success of the series "can be attributed to its themes of mortgage slavery, corruption, and the pitfalls inherent to China's economic boom" (2016: 3). For Zurndorfer, the series alludes to the new sexual economy of China, which "is dominated by wealthy and politically influential men who consume femininity and sexuality. In exchange, women receive material comfort and financial security. But, this is not an equal exchange" (2016: 4–5). In a country that is so much taken by commercialization and consumption, love and gender are deeply entrenched in a sexual economy. Masculinity is articulated along the lines of being a successful businessman, while women "view their bodies as valuable commodities to be exchanged for income and security" (2016: 6). Gender roles are thus reinforced, producing inequalities in which men hold a privileged position and women are objectified and meant to serve. This leads Zurndorfer to observe that "Young Chinese women are in a no-win situation. If they develop themselves and earn enough to live independently, they are condemned for their ambitions. In contrast, if they seek a successful man, they are labeled 'gray' " (2016: 16). As our examples later will show, there are other and somehow more hopeful sexual economies proliferating as well in China.

When we visited the Love Club in Beijing on a foggy Friday night in November 2015, to attend a seminar by the love guru Zhao Yunjiu, we were surprised to see people of different ages, ranging from their early 20s to their 50s, and with different status – some came as a couple, others were single. Zhao is the writer of various self-help books on love. With his soft spoken voice he calmly presents his views on love and relationships to his admiring audience. During the seminar we were struck by the openness of the questions from the audience. One woman explained she did not know how to express her love to a man she admired for a long time, while another woman explained how she and her partner were having troubles in love. In her study on the Love Club in Shanghai, Pi Chenying shows how the three-month training program, costing 4500 yuan, stimulates women to produce a "daring and desiring self," who takes more distance from the opinions of parents, who experiments sexually, and who sets clear goals for the future. As Pi writes (2016), "independence, emotionality, and socializing skills become competences and thus need to be cultivated. Women not only can, but more importantly *should*, play more active roles, i.e. actively transforming the self." The emergence of love clubs in cities in China, and the related popularity of self-help publications, is indicative of the emergence of a therapeutic culture in China, which in turn can be associated with what Eva Illouz has called "emotional capitalism" that is underpinning the global spread of therapeutic culture (Illouz 2007).

A final example to illustrate the importance of a heterosexual marriage comes from a visit to a park in Shanghai. A Sunday visit to the People's Park is unlikely to be solely relaxing. One will find hundreds of parents and grandparents with a board presenting their (grand-) children, mostly female, including information about age, education, height, and occasionally zodiac sign, income, and personality. This "marriage market" that takes place every weekend indexes not only the importance of familism as we mentioned in chapter 1 but also that of the governmentalities over marriage, presenting an interesting scenario of the juxtaposition of free partner choice and arranged marriage – as the market somehow connects both. There are different displays at different corners of the park. For example, one corner focuses in particular on men and women who have studied abroad. The respective flags of different countries order these posts and make it easier for the viewer to navigate. Whether or not these markets are successful, and to what extent they actually serve as a socializing space for the parents and grandparents is hard to say, but they do attest to the importance attached to being married – and preferably before the age of 30 – and above all the potency of governmentality over proper gender and sexuality performances.

Our analysis so far has presented a diverse array of cultural practices – ranging from statistical studies to television dating shows, and love clubs to marriage parks – through which heteronormative discourses are being maintained and sustained. In the remainder of this chapter we will look at three different domains that may help unsettle this discourse: romance comedy, queer culture, and sexual cultures.

UNSETTLING HETERONORMATIVITY I: ROMANCE COMEDY

In recent years, numerous romantic comedies have become widely popular in Chinese cinema. One of them is *Love Is Not Blind* (2011), directed by Huatao Teng, a 1995 graduate from the Beijing Film Academy. He is best known for his television dramas that depict the lives and loves of young urbanites in China. While we are aware that such bestselling movies tend to promote a heteronormative discourse, we would also like to show that even then, there are openings for something different – in this case, the movie is not quite straight, nor is it quite gay.

The movie is based on an online novel by Bao Jingjing, who claimed to use interviews with young people for the project. After a little over one week of its release, *Love Is Not Blind* – which cost only 9 million yuan (US$1.4 million) to make – had earned over 200 million yuan (approximately US$31.5 million) at the box office. The film was released on November 8 in response to the date 11/11/2011, which was hailed as China's singles' day. The film depicts 33 days (indeed: 11+11+11) in the life of lead protagonist Huang Xiaoxian, a 27-year-old woman, who just broke up with her boyfriend after watching him shopping intimately with her best friend. At this time, she receives the full support of her co-worker Wang Yiyang, a very gayish male character.

One review proclaims that the movie "strives to comfort and warm the hearts of all those individuals who celebrate Singles Day" (Chen 2011). Set in an impeccably clean Beijing, with the main characters living in beautifully decorated shiny apartments and working for a fancy wedding planner organization, the movie portrays Huang Xiao-xian in her "recovery" from the break-up. In particular, her interaction with witty, ironic, and yet supportive Wang Yiyang drives the plot forward. As one review proclaims, "even though Yiyang's sexual orientation is never explicitly mentioned in the film, the film is essentially about the importance of having a non-threatening male in your life. That alone makes *Love Is Not Blind* a refreshing change from the usual romantic comedy" (Ma 2011). The movie can thus also be read as an ode to friendship, that may be a longer-lasting force in life than romantic love, and as such challenges heteronormative celebrations of coupledom.

And the movie does so in particular connection with coupledom's symbiosis with consumer culture in contemporary urban China. The opening scene presents different ways to split up for a couple in differ-ent but similar spaces: modern Beijing with its shiny tall buildings, fancy bars, artistic districts, and luxuriously modernistic apartments. This is the new modern "purified" Beijing against the backdrop of con-spicuous consumption of brand labels and sumptuousness of food in the restaurants opened by star painters like Fang Lijun. It is in a luxuri-ous shopping mall where Xiaoxian comes across her boyfriend Lu Ran selecting perfume with another woman. Ironically, this breaking-up scene seems to be suggesting that while the capitalistic society is urging us to buy and give presents, for instance, on Valentine's Day, the act of consumption may also break apart a relationship. It is the start of Xiaoxian being single, a state of despair and loss, a state in which the support of her male colleague Yiyang becomes indispensable.

Such ambivalence toward the co-construction of heteronormativity and consumerism continues throughout the movie. When the two lead characters are asked to arrange the wedding of a super-rich couple – emblematic of the new rich of China, Miss Li and Mr Wei, they meet up for high tea. Li presents them with her wedding ring and asks: "isn't my engagement ring beautiful?" to which Xiaoxian replies "Very beautiful, must be really expensive." "It's from Tiffany," Li responds. Later on, it turns out that the two lead characters cannot comply with all the wishes of the couple and thus quit the assignment. However, Xiaoxian continues to meet Wei, and in a park she confronts him with his partner choice. The critique on consumption is articulated most directly in this scene. She asks Wei,

> Many great guys date girls who always talk about Louis Vuitton and Prada. If you talk about the essence of love, she'll most likely tell you that the limit you set on her credit card is the essence of your love for her. Why? Why is there such a match?

In response, Wei replies,

> Two words: save trouble. We want to find wives who can stick with us even when love fades away. Can you accept it? Li Ke can. For her, love is a luxury, but LV is a necessity. For girls like you, LV is a luxury, but love is a necessity. The LV group won't suddenly go bankrupt, but love can end in a minute. If I want to build a relationship, I have to make

sure I have endless resources to supply it. From that perspective I'm a very dependable man.

On the one hand, the movie presents a sanitized city in which middle- and upper-class young people live lavishly; on the other, it problematizes the very excessiveness of consumption and the commodification of heteronormative coupledom.

We hasten to add that the critique on consumerism that *Love Is Not Blind* offers remains quite paradoxical. To begin with, the entire environment shown in the movie and its consumption culture make it hard for audiences to take the critique on conspicuous consumption all too seriously. The movie also makes the flip side of the city invisible; there is no appearance of migrant workers that make all these fancy shopping malls possible, no pollution from the factories and cars, no dust from the coal mines.

Finally the movie addresses the ultimate question of the durability of marriage and of love. It turns out that the message is: the dream wedding may not be a dream after all; love may be ending. What is suggested in the finale of the movie is that friendship lasts longer, as the friendship between the single woman Xiaoxian and the gayish man Yiyang continues to prosper. This unlikely couple – unlikely in a romantic comedy and unlikely in real life – may not be fundamentally undermining the heteronormative framing of the movie; after all, heterosexual relationships remain the norm, the dream. It does, however, propagate a politics of friendship that can hold this unsettling potential when we push it further. In the final scene, we see Xiaoxian gazing out of the window of her fancy office located next to the Village, the most glamorous shopping district in Beijing. She looks at a neon light that seems not to be working. Suddenly her cell phone rings. It is Yiyang, asking her to look closer at the neon light, and the word "faith" appears. And then, Yiyang says, "No matter what happens. I will be around." It is a final affirmation of the importance of friendships in our lives, amidst all the disappointments of heterosexual love.

UNSETTLING HETERONORMATIVITY II: QUEER CHINA

Yiyang, the gayish character, in *Love Is Not Blind* is typical of the *gaymi*: a term referring to the gay best friend of (single) women. While he attests to the increased visibility of queer culture in mainstream Chinese media, the refusal to frame him as gay is quite telling. He also fits in a long tradition of cinematic negotiations with homosexuality in Chinese cinema in which we can often witness a play with gender and sexuality, rather than a clear proclamation of one's sexual preference. Since the 1990s there has been a steady rise of a queer cinema circulating in and among China, Taiwan, and Hong Kong (Leung 2008; Lim 2006). Rather than a clear politics of coming out, Chinese cinema often searches for different, less visible, paths. Often these are queer stories that are "half-heard and dimly remembered that circulate in the nooks and crannies of daily life" (Leung 2008: 3), they constitute an "undercurrent," to use Helen Leung's term, that may be the most evocative and most promising for articulating a "queer" politics. In such discourses and cinematic representations, as seen, for example, in the movies of Tsai Ming-liang, there is a move away, rather than toward, identity – which unsettles heteronormative discourse that is so much grounded in the idea of the sexual self.

The history of homosexuality in China can be traced back to imperial times, where a rich tradition of homosexual acts has been documented. Understanding the queer formation revolves not around an innate sexual essence or a sexual identity, but is rather contingent on actions, tendencies, and preferences (Geyer 2002; Hinsch 1990; Wei 2007). Over the past decades the discourse changed rapidly, introducing different terms that refer to homosexuality. While the more formal

Chinese term is *tongxinglian*, literally same-sex love, numerous other terms have proliferated. One of the first terms, *tongzhi* (comrade), was appropriated from communist China under which members used this de-gendered and revolutionary term to address each other. It was first used in the 1970s by a Hong Kong cultural critic Maike and later in 1989 formally adopted by a Hong Kong cultural personality Edward Lam for the Hong Kong gay and lesbian film festival. Since then, *nütongzhi* (lesbian) and *nantongzhi* (gay) have remained in currency. The term has also come to stand for a non-confrontational mode of being gay; what matters then is safeguarding one's social role at the expense of proclaiming its sexual attitude. This can be read as an alternative to identity politics that insists on coming out, and as such has been hailed by some as a Chinese way of being gay (Coleman and Chou 2000). Kam (2013: 12) refers to this non-confrontational alternative as a "politics of public correctness" that refers to "a logic of normalization that seeks to promote a 'healthy' and 'proper' image of *tongzhi* in order to acquire social and familial recognition, developed as a response to the changing forms of oppression and opportunity of *tongzhi* during the reform era." Kam rightly points at the potential violence it does to personal lives, as it deprives homosexual subjects of a speaking position.

As Engebretsen explains in her monograph on queer women in China, the term *tongzhi*, while being gender neutral, has come to refer more to gay men than lesbian women. It is, in addition, perilous to read this label as denoting a unique, indigenous Chinese gay identity; that would smack of a sexual essentialism that would do injustice to the complex local, national, and global entanglements through which gay and lesbian subjectivities emerge in China. By now the term is increasingly being replaced by other terms in post-millennium China, like *lala*, gay, queer (*ku'er*), and the acronym LGBT (lesbian, gay, bisexual, transgender) has become more common – all these refer to "systems of collective markers rather than a straightforward description of homogeneous groups of people of fixed sexual identity" (Engebretsen 2015: xv). These terms broaden people's imagination over gender social realities and communities, but by the same token they also run the danger of becoming disciplinary terms that shape and limit people's experiences. There are also terms that are more locally specific. For example, local people in Chengdu, a city in southwest China, called homosexual men "wandering man" (*piao piao*), alluding to their floating around without root or anchor (Wei 2007: 574).

Significantly, as seen from the characterization of Yiyang in *Love Is Not Blind*, being gay in China has shifted from a discourse of deviance to a type of urban and cultural citizenship that "emphasizes quality, individuality, difference and modernity" (Kong 2010: 12). Moreover, we witness a wider range of subject positions, as also becomes clear from Lucetta Kam's study on *lala*, or lesbians, in Shanghai (2013). This ethnographic account of *lala* communities presents their struggles not only with hegemonic heteronormative ideologies that operate in conjunction with strong familial pressures but also with the already mentioned politics of public correctness. The study shows, however, how *lala* increasingly carve out their own space in the city, and in their lives, and develop different strategies in resisting heteronormative demands.

Aside from terminological and discursive formations and transformations, the past decades have witnessed an emergence of queer cultures in the bigger cities in China in the form of bars, dance clubs, private parties, and numerous websites and apps for dating. This not only has facilitated new dating, playing, and sexual practices, it has also made Chinese queer culture more and more part of a global queer culture. In a show by Taiwanese pop singer A Mei in Beijing on October 11, 2015, the inner circle of the stadium was filled with rainbow flags. Before she started to sing her song "Rainbow," A Mei said: "This is the first time I've ever seen so many rainbow flags, thank you!" (Youku 2015). A Mei then held up her own rainbow flag, written on which was Beijing in Chinese characters. This openness was quite unthinkable a decade ago. It must be noted that the tickets for the inner ring were sold by the gay dating app Blued, pointing to the connection between queer culture and commercial culture. The Pink renminbi is gaining power in China; such tickets are only affordable for the affluent class. Such open performances of queerness also contradict the earlier mentioned withdrawal from identitarian labels that characterized gay culture in China until recently. It shows that labels like *tongzhi* or LGBT alone fail to capture the complexity of queer lives in China, neither does the dichotomy of coming out or not coming out help us very much. We would like to present briefly four examples of this complexity, linking each to respective governmental logics.

Our first example is cosplay (a portmanteau from costume play, where participants dress to represent specific characters from popular culture). Chinese media, in particular new media, increasingly tolerate more extreme or daring gender performances because of the market demand. We interviewed in Hangzhou the 304 ACG Society, basically a BL (boys' love, a term borrowed from Japanese manga culture) cosplay club, the male members of which are known for cosplaying female characters in Chinese comics. Long, bright-colored hair, heavy girlish make-up and long robes are characteristics of these cosplay figures. The ambiguity of gender represented by the 304 Society is so popular that it won many cosplay awards organized in the major cities of China (e.g. Hangzhou National ACG Festival, Shanghai Cartoon Festival organized by Shanghai Media Group, and China's National ACG Cosplay contest). They are then invited by many famous brands, from wedding to jewelry companies, to appear at various media events to sell their products. Needless to say, their performances are always already enmeshed in a complex web of power, money, and sex. Neither are the gender-image-reversed boys, at least according to our interviews, innocent, nor are they neutral about their gender representation – their performance can also be related to the *demand* in society to express

Image 5. Cosplayer at the China International Cartoon and Animation Festival 2015 in Hangzhou (photo by Anthony Fung)

one's gendered self, and the better they perform the female gender, the better they are.

In our study of the 304 Society, the male-turned-female cosplayers all have to conform to such logics of gender and sexuality. Thus, when we interviewed two of the cosplayers in a regular restaurant in downtown Hangzhou, they all dressed in "normal" T-shirt and trousers with all their feminine, soft, and sensual gestures hidden. However, similar to the young migrant workers we will discuss in chapter 5, technologies of self are at work, meaning that these cosplayers apply their techniques of cosplay make-up to their body, and create new norms and relationships with the governmental logics. Their subversive potentials toward heteronormative constructions of, in this case, masculinity, are reflected in the occasional hostility from media coverage (see Chow forthcoming on another cosplay group Ailisi). Their transgender practices evolve into new rules that circulate and are being circulated on their body, although in daily life, society, and public, there is no attempt for them to intervene in the governmental logic of the state and other institutions. Their new cultural logics, if not resistance, have become popular among the youth, and ironically, companies as well as the authorities sometimes have to "co-opt" them to perform in public to draw other youngsters' attention and stimulate consumption.

Our second example is marriage of convenience. Many gay men and lesbian women do marry someone of the opposite sex, often without letting their spouses know their sexual preference. However, over the past decade, with the support of new technologies, an alternative has emerged: there are now dating websites where gay men and lesbian woman look for each other and engage in a (fake or cooperative) wedding to pacify the parents, while being able to continue a gay lifestyle aside from their marriage (Kam 2013). In the 2013 documentary *Our Marriages*, filmmakers He Xiaopei and Yuan Yuan follow four lesbian women who set out to marry gay men in order to pacify their families. The four women in the documentary live together, their gay spouses – found through a website – live elsewhere. In the documentary we see how the women are struggling to find a suitable gay spouse, while keeping their own relationship in place as well. But meanwhile, they laugh, make jokes, and reflect in a quite light-hearted way on their predicament. Rather than being portrayed as victims of a hetero-normative system, the women take pleasure in their bending of the rules, laugh about their wedding dress, and make fun of the wedding banquet.

Indeed, despite the fact that the "coming out" phenomenon is more common these days, as suggested by Wei Wei's study (2007: 579), many gay and lesbian Chinese expressed that the very act or insistence on homosexuality should not jeopardize marriage and family, the two very institutional practices strongly rooted in Chinese society. What these marriages of convenience lay bare is that while the governmental power of the family, as we discussed in chapter 1, remains in place, it is queered at the same time. The wedding banquet is queered by the presence of gay friends, just as the couple queers expectations of what constitutes a good marriage as they do not even live together, often condoned by their families. Rather than simply dismissing such marriages as a hypocritical act, a fooling and coping tactic, we also read them as a subversion of the institution and conventions of marriage itself, a bending of the heteronormative rules.

In any case, these marriages of convenience should not erase some other attempts to push the boundaries of legal and social acceptance. For instance, as part of an emerging LGBT activism, gay marriages are being performed in public and online. In January 2016, a gay couple in Changsha went to court to sue the local government for not allowing them to get married. The court has accepted to take on this first case of same-sex marriage. These examples show that while for some, a marriage of convenience is a queer way to pacify the family, others opt for a more open and confrontational mode in their wish to change the system.

Third, in the cinema of directors like Cui Zi'en, He Xiaopei, and Fan Popo, we witness a similar direct queer aesthetics that seems a far cry from the more subdued and much less articulate cinema from, for example, Tsai Mingliang. Fan Popo is not only an activist-director of numerous documentaries but also the director of the Beijing queer film festival, which since its beginnings in 2001 leads a very uncertain existence and is often banned by the government. Born in 1985, his approach is media savvy, entangled with the global LGBT movement and advocates acceptance of queer people in a more open and diverse society. In 2015, Fan Popo sued the state, more precisely the State Administration of Press, Publication, Radio, Film and Television, for taking his documentary *Mama Rainbow* offline. The documentary is dedicated to mothers of gay children, who give talks at universities to express their support for the LGBT movement. To his own surprise, Fan won the case. But, as he explained to us in February 2016, so far the documentary still has not reappeared online.

In his movies, Fan Popo is clearly an exponent of a global (that is, predominantly Western) LGBT discourse. The supporting text of *Mama Rainbow* on the DVD claims that they "talk openly and freely about their experiences with their gay and lesbian children. With their love, they are giving a whole new definition to Chinese-style family bonds." In *Be a Woman*, Fan explores the drag queen scene in Nanning, a city located in northwestern China. His turn towards a more activist mode of filmmaking was triggered in 2005, as he explains (interview on February 4, 2016):

> When I was studying film I thought I would make movies just for myself. But this changed for me when the Beijing Queer Film Festival was shut down at Peking University in 2005. I felt very angry, and felt I should do something to change this.

While he feels uncomfortable being labeled a queer filmmaker, Fan also understands why he is not simply called a filmmaker. There are only a handful of people making queer movies in China. This hints at the complexity of such labels; they are needed in order to carve out a space of expression, yet at the same time they are limiting and confining. In a public debate on queer cultures in China in Beijing on March 28,

2016, Fan Popo expressed the reaction of his father to his work, who expressed concern over his activist stance:

> I am from a very rural area in China…My dad is from the generation of the Cultural Revolution and he also experienced the Tiananmen Square events, he is very negative about anything related to politics.

His words attest to the generational differences discussed in chapter 1. Fan's work helps to undermine the dominant heterosexual culture, unpack the diversity of queer subcultures in China, and give a voice to those that remain silenced often. As we remarked earlier, the question whether such visibility is necessarily liberating remains open.

Fourth, the emergence of dating apps has not only contributed to a vibrant sexual culture; it has also fuelled a desire for more visibility – as our example of the A Mei concert with the rainbow flags attests to. To sustain their position in a highly competitive online market, the apps are involved in many related activities, such as gay tourism, arranging overseas same-sex marriage, selling tickets to concerts and parties, massage, as well as the production and distribution of online drama. These drama series – for example *Rainbow Family* (*yiwu zanke*) and *Me and Mr X* (*wo gen X xiansheng*), are not only attractive to gay audiences, but also to young people, in particular girls. In their playfulness, these movies are a far cry from the works of Fan Popo. The drama series generally feature young, sexy boys – for which the term "new fresh meat" (*xiaoxianrou*) has become the generic label. In 2016, Blued launched the short movie "My 17 gay friends" (*wode 17 ge ji you gaosu ni GAY quan "you duo luan"*) directed by Moxie Peng. The short movie presents the dating culture of a group of gay people. The opening lines are indicative of the directness of the movie, as it introduces the character Li Mo, while showing his partly naked body in suggestive poses, with a voiceover narrating:

This is my friend Li Mo, tall and very handsome. Because he is a big, tall guy, many people think he is a "1" (top), 1 means stick, in Chinese gay circles it represents the dominant side. But Li Mo is really a "0" (bottom). That's the "hole," the passive side. Because he is often mistaken as a top and because he wants to save face, Li Mo is forced to claim he is a 0.5 to others. 0.5, as the name implies, means versatile. (Peng 2016)

The characters, mostly Chinese, some white, one black, are all young and pretty and well dressed. We are presented here with the affluent urban elites of China – not unlike those in *Love Is Not Blind* – that are likely to work in either the creative industries or the finance sector, use Apple computers, and spend their free time in fancy bars drinking coffee and wine. While, on the one hand, we can read the movie as a sign of the sexual opening up of China, on the other hand, it promotes a middle-class subjectivity that only few people can afford. In addition, all stories revolve around the desire for a relationship, thus affirming the normativity if not cult of the couple. While movies like this do present Chinese audiences with alternatives to heteronormative discourses, it does not make them necessarily less normative – what they produce is a desiring neoliberal self (Rofel 2007).

While in general these online series manage to skillfully evade censorship, some are less lucky. For example, *Addiction* was taken from the major Chinese streaming sites in January 2016. The series consisting of 15 episodes focuses on what is termed BL romances between four high school students. The series, made by a Beijing-based production house, became an instant success and was viewed over 10 million times on the day after it premiered (Lin and Chen 2016). The comments that were posted on *Weibo* following the ban are indicative of how censorship also produces discourse, sometimes unsettling rather than affirming heteronormative discourse. Shortly after the ban of the series, we analyzed posts on *Weibo* commenting on the ban. They expressed anger and annoyance about this ban:

> #Addiction is banned# I have been waited too long for the update of Addiction only to find that it is banned. Even using up all the bad language I have learnt my life can't express my hate for the State Administration of Press, Publication, Radio, Film and Television. (http://weibo.com/2609545921/Dj4ZkaBMz?from=page _1005052609545921_profile&wvr=6&mod=weibotime&type =comment, retrieved March 6, 2016)

> We watched Addiction. You said the characters' names are related to drugs and the topic is gay so you banned it. Hahaha what do you want us to watch? CCTV news or weather report for 24 hours a day? You are lower and lower. (http://weibo.com/5256853721/Dkr QH5HNQ?from=page_1005055256853721_profile&wvr=6 &mod=weibotime&type=comment, retrieved March 6, 2016)

These comments not only attest to the importance of social media platforms for constituting a space where a meta-discourse on the production (and censoring) of culture takes place, they also show how media-savvy audiences are triggered into subject positions that express anger and annoyance towards the authorities.

To summarize from the four examples cited above, they illustrate the diversity and multiplicity of queer cultures in China. While they help unsettle, some more, some less, the heteronormative discourses that permeate society, they are also part and parcel of a governmental logic, driven for example by notions like "freedom" and "emancipation," notions that, as we argued before, also have disciplinary implications. They often validate the cult of the couple, or they celebrate a luxurious middle-class urban lifestyle; in doing so, they draw new boundaries, promote specific modes of subjectivity, while disavowing other modes, or rendering them simply impossible. What about, for example, the gay or lesbian migrant worker or farmer? What about the people that do not like sex at all? What about feelings of missing out in the race toward a luxurious lifestyle, for those who do not manage to secure well-paid jobs that are needed to sustain such a lifestyle? These questions are skillfully circumvented in the cultural practices that we have analyzed.

UNSETTLING HETERONORMATIVITY III: SEX AND FEMINISM

Over the past decades, sexuality has long been relegated to the area of reproductive rights and concerns, as attested by the ubiquitous presence of contraceptives in stores in China and the implementation of the one child policy. Nevertheless, like anywhere else, sex remains also a highly sensitive and contested issue. In the words of Zhang Qingfei, "sexuality has been a taboo in the Confucian Chinese society for its close association with morality. Especially when socialist ideologies were incorporated into Confucian culture, lust was viewed as a bourgeois element that threatened spiritual purity and socialist order" (2015: 89). Socialism is constructed as asexual, capitalism as sexual, reinforcing stereotypes along the lines of "you stress sex, we stress family." This narrative has been increasingly punctured over the past decades.

James Farrer, for example, analyzes how during the 1990s the rapid modernization of Shanghai with its discos and clubs triggered a reform of youth's romantic and sex culture. As we have seen earlier, dating and sex before marriage have become more common, and there is a greater freedom to change partner. Farrer analyzes how Shanghai youth balance the contradictions of a China in reform, when he writes:

> In order to cope with the contradictions and conflicting goals of this new liberal market environment, Shanghai youth employ a loosely

ordered repertoire of contemporary codes that balance one attitude with its opposite. Young women, anxious to be both pragmatic and pure of heart, rhetorically balance "conditions" with "feelings." Young people wishing to engage in premarital sex redefine intercourse as an expression of love. Finally, youth evade the inherent contradictions between romantic commitments and an ideal of free choice through a consumption-oriented discourse of play in which dating relationships can be described as "just for fun." (2002: 14)

Youth construct stories to resolve contradictions between morality and sexuality. Some, however, quite univocally claim the latter terrain, especially female writers. Two prominent voices are Mian Mian, author of *Lalala* and *Candy*, and Wei Hui, author of *Shanghai Baby*. Both authors became front-page news in the late 1990s with their daring novels in which sex, drugs, and rock'n'roll constituted the main components. They were hailed internationally as being at the forefront of China's sexual reform. At the same time, the explicit sex scenes, the indulgence of the female characters in carnal pleasure, also mark a shift towards consumerism and its underpinning ideology of individualism, free choice, and hedonism (Scheen 2015). While these antidotes can be regarded as an alternative to the conventions for women's writing, they are formulated to "reify the divide between the body and the mind and situate women on one side of this existing binary, namely that of the body" (Zhong 2006: 655). Here, we outline two articulations of sexual cultures and youth in China in their entanglements with heteronormative discourse.

Role of new media

One of the biggest changes in China since the 1990s is undoubtedly the rapid introduction of the Internet and social media platforms.

The emergence of online cultures presents a unique opportunity for Chinese youth to plug into, and become part of, a worldwide sex and dating culture. Katrien Jacobs' book on *People's Pornography* presents a study of the connection between sex and the Internet in China. She rightly notes how new media technologies both enable and disable the proliferation of sexual cultures, as they can be and are also being used by the state as a mode of surveillance. Her book explores the works of female sex bloggers like Mu Zimei and Hairong Tian Tian, whose explicit blogs were later also published as books. In the format of a reality show, they offered followers a glimpse of a sexual lifestyle hitherto censored. Jacobs shows how as a response, "a sensibility of intolerance and moral arrogance shapes itself around their digital provocations" (2012: 21).

While Jacobs' study maps out the changes taking place, they run the aforementioned danger of becoming complicit with equating the opening up of China with more sexual freedom. Farrer makes the same observation when he writes that the narrative of opening up is "a dominant feature of a local rhetoric of cultural change.... What matters most from my account is how these terms are used to mark moral and social boundaries in a newly forming market society" (Farrer 2002: 12). As he claims, "My account of a changing sexual culture is not a story of sexual liberation, sexual globalization, or rebelling youth, but of youth collectively constructing (and individually coping with) a new culture of sexual choice, publicly articulated through a dramatistic rhetoric of motives" (Farrer 2002: 19). "New" sexual modes and new dating practices will continue to be ridden with power relations that intersect with class, gender, and age. Rather than celebrating an assumed opening up of China and China's youth, it seems more urgent to probe into these modes of inclusion and exclusion, as well as to question their alleged artificial newness, as past moralities often seep through what are claimed to be new moralities.

At the other extreme, so to speak, the Internet constitutes the platforms for asexual people to get to know each other. In her study of the asexual movement in China, Day Wong shows that the pressure to marry also haunts Chinese with little or no interest in sex. Our observations earlier about marriages of convenience between lesbians and gays are also relevant for the way Chinese asexuals manage their life. The website wx920.com serves as the dating platform for the asexual population. "Wx920 expanded rapidly and claims to have nearly 200,000 members, and to have facilitated over 23,000 successful matches to date. In addition to asexuals, it also targets homosexuals who want sexless marriages in order to pass as heterosexual couples" (Wong 2015: 104). Asexuality undermines the heterosexual matrix; it challenges the importance attached to sex – an importance that generally remains uncontested in LGBT discourse. Wong (2015: 106) quotes two of her informants, saying that:

> I couldn't give her what she needed. What normal woman wouldn't need sex? Even though she didn't say it, I could see that this was the case. I just couldn't bear to ruin her life. (XF, male, 23)

> I don't want to hurt a normal man, that's why I hope to find a partner here…I dated someone before, but I was unwilling to hurt him and broke up with him. I was unable to satisfy him sexually. If you love a person, you can't bear to leave him unfulfilled sexually for his whole life. (CH, female, 31)

The discourse of normality remains largely in place, when asexuals define their lack of desire as something abnormal, and to give sexual happiness is framed as an ethical duty (Wong 2015: 106). Negotiating these norms, however, asexuals in China connect through the Internet, not only for finding a partner, but also for support. That some opt for a marriage underlines once again the power of the family in Chinese culture.

Feminist activism and the Vagina Monologues

We opened this chapter referring to the detainment of five feminist activists in the spring of 2015. Feminism has, of course, a long history in China itself (Croll 2013 [1978]). Recent years have witnessed an upsurge in public activism, and Fan Popo's documentary *The VaChina Monologues* offers a unique glimpse of it. The documentary follows the adaptations of the *Vagina Monologues* in Chinese cities, the first of which took place in Guangzhou in December 2003. Wu Xiao-yan recalls in the documentary:

> I really liked the atmosphere back then. We were just a bunch of girls chatting about topics you wouldn't normally talk about, like sexual harassment and menstruation. In 2005 my act was "angry vagina." That's a far cry from my personality back then. I was a really nice girl before then, I gave people that impression.

In Beijing, the play was titled *Our Vaginas, Our Selves* (*Yin dao Zhi dao*), performed in June 2013. The title is a wordplay on the concept *dao*, as actress Ai Ke explains…

> "*Zhi dao*" because it's vagina's (*yindao*) way (*dao*), and because *dao* is a very Chinese concept, *dao*, it's reason, it's principle, it's a way, etcetera. So vagina's *dao* is meaningful both in its form and its content. Also because "*zhi dao*" is phonetically the same as the word for "know." So it also represents the vagina as representative of female subjectivity, as in "Vagina Knows."

These performances spilled over to other public realms. Young women would walk in the Beijing subway for a "short skirt flash mob" against sexual harassment, proclaiming that "my short skirt is not an invitation or a provocation, it's not an indication that I want it or give it." The performances of *Vagina Monologues* and the public activist interventions show how Chinese youth at times do transgress boundaries and challenge dominant constructions of proper womanhood and heteronormative practices. In an interview with us on March 27, 2016, Wei Tingting explained how today's feminist activism is different:

> The mode of activism becomes different from the previous generation, which is also linked to the changes in the civil society in China. Particularly the performance action…such as the Occupy Male Toilet action by some young feminists.

Instead of protesting, the new generation do public performances, which makes it more difficult for the state to intervene, and also the media find it easier and more interesting to cover these, she explained to us. Only when the performances became organized in different cities, as in March 2015, did the authorities intervene, resulting in their detention; hence their discontent, if not fear, about the shrinking mediascape and about the tightening of control and censorship under the leadership of Xi Jinping. While the Internet has opened up avenues for new sexual and asexual cultures usually silenced by heteronormative ideals, and feminist theater and activism challenge patriarchal norms in Chinese society, the pace and even direction of change remain unclear.

CONCLUSION

China's opening up turns out to be a hazardous, messy, and ambiguous process when it comes to gender, sexuality, and love. We have shown how a heteronormative discourse remains firmly in place, underpinned by neo-Confucian ideologies and the importance attached to the family. The family produces a mode of belonging not just to one's spouse, but also to the nation-state and to Chinese culture (Rofel 2007). We have explored Chinese heteronormativity through an analysis of dating shows on television, marriage parks in Shanghai, numerous studies related to the sex life of Chinese youth, and the sexual economy that continues to privilege men. We continued to look for unsettling discourses, and have shown how in romance comedy, a politics of friendship is propagated above marriage and love. Queer cultures present a more direct challenge to heteronormativity, as we have shown in our analysis of the cosplay groups, marriages of convenience, queer cinema, and the popularity of Internet dramas, in conjunction with apps like Blued and ZANK. Finally, focusing on sex and feminism, we analyzed the role of the Internet on sexuality and the appropriation of the *Vagina Monologues* and related articulations of feminist activism in public space.

All these practices constitute and are constituted by the multiplicity of sex, gender, and love in contemporary China. We have analyzed profound changes that allow for experimentations with new sexualities, new forms of dating, and new modes of relationship between same gender partners, changes in which new media often play a crucial enabling role. Having said that, we have also tried to caution against a too celebratory account. As we have illustrated in different domains, all these new spaces are mostly parasitic on the existing infrastructure, social institutions, and state apparatus. These allegedly new possibilities often carry the burden of the past, in which marriage, heteronormativity, and family values play a pivotal role; they are also always already entangled in complex power relationships, in which the classical sociological demographic variables continue to produce significant fault lines, underpinned by a specific political economy that warrants further scrutiny. The role of dating apps is of particular interest here, as they capitalize on China's sexual economy, and promote a lifestyle that smacks of middle-class values and aesthetics, pushing aside questions of social inequality. The modern gendered and sexed subjectivities are enmeshed in a complex web of power, the possibility to come out as gay can well become an imperative, disavowing other possibilities of leading a queer life, just as Internet pornography may well sustain rather than challenge unequal gender roles. Furthermore, with the emergence of a wider range of subjectivities youth can experiment with, the burden to explore one's desiring self also increases, a desiring self that is deeply implicated in and complicit with China's state-promoted market economy.

5 Mobility, Marginalization, and Desire

I came to this company for money. [But then I realized], this is a waste of my life and my future. In the first step of my adult life, I took the wrong path. I'm lost.

Lu Xin (in Chan and Pun 2010: 27)

INTRODUCTION

In 2009, the year between the Beijing Olympics and the Shanghai Expo, Lu Xin moved from his hometown in Hunan province to Shenzhen, where he worked for the Foxconn factory. As a graduate from university, he earned RMB2,000 monthly, more than double the pay of the line workers. Working extensive overtime, he still managed to wire RMB13,000 back to his family over a period of eight months of hard work there. On October 26, 2009, he posted the statement with which we open this chapter on his blog. In April 2010, he worked around 12 hours a day. Another post was added on March 14, 2010, which reads "If I really could, I'd write music every day. I don't have money [to buy] music hardware equipment. I don't even want to spend money on a computer. I can't find a record company either. Youth flies away. The 24 years old of me, can I still do it?" (Chan and Pun 2010: 27). Despite being the runner-up in a company singing contest, his daily life is simply composed of monotonous tasks in the assembly workshop of the factory that supplies the world with, among other items, iPhones, computers, and tablets. He became extremely unhappy, feeling devastated and desperate one sleepless day in early May. His university classmate and co-worker recalled what happened: "He said he was going to look at the scenery and right after he finished his sentence, he quickly opened the window and jumped onto the balcony, then jumped off from the balcony. He never hesitated. I tried to grab him, but only pulled the clothes on his left arm, he threw my hand off" (Chan and Pun 2010: 28). Lu Xin jumped from the sixth floor at the age of 24 on May 6, 2010.

The sad story is retold in a moving piece written by Jenny Chan and Pun Ngai titled "Suicide as Protest for the New Generation of Chinese Migrant Workers: Foxconn, Global Capital and the State" (2010). In the article, the authors analyze the events of spring 2010, during which 13 young workers attempted or committed suicide at the two Foxconn production facilities in southern China. Critiquing the attempts of the factory to trivialize the suicides, they interpret these acts as protest against an unjust global labor regime, in which leading international brands, factory management, and local officials are deeply implicated. The rise of China, so much celebrated during both the Beijing Olympics and the Shanghai Expo, comes at a price, and it is often youth that have to pay this price.

A celebration of China's youth as being at the forefront of change, immersing themselves in trendy urban lifestyles, and paving the way for a more open and more prosperous China presents, to say the least, a naïve and biased account. In our other chapters we focus on how Chinese youth navigate between the possible and the impossible, between a politics of probability and a politics of possibility (see Appadurai 2013). In this chapter, we will take a closer look at a particular group of youth that is often marginalized: the migrant youth that leave the countryside to go to big cities to pursue a dream of a better future, and soon find that it is only a broken dream. Currently there are an estimated 250 million migrant workers in China with 13 million adding to this legion annually. They can be seen as the flip side of the glamour of urbanism, industrialization, the growing socialist market economy, and China's rising global trade. Studies show that youth account for a significant portion of this population as one would readily expect youth to have strong physical power and to be less tolerant of the mundane life in the village. It is estimated that those between 15 and 35 years of age make up around 70 percent of the rural–urban migrants (Hays 2015). For a long time, these workers "floated" to Beijing, Shanghai, Guangzhou, Shenzhen, and other coastal cities, but more and more are now driven to the interior and western part of China with tides of China's factories retreating inland.

Departing largely from the ideal of the youth worker during the early formation of the Communist Party by its cofounder Chen Duxiu – who suggested youth workers should take the dual role of improving youth farmers' lives and develop the revolutionary spirit of the class in the Communist Youth League's first National Congress in Guangzhou in 1922 – youth workers, in particular the factory and migrant workers, are deprived of basic rights, nor are they included in Xi Jinping's "China Dream." Now the youth born in the rural areas are waiting in vain for better times, or they grow up in abandoned industrial areas. The trickle-down effect never comes; their waiting for prosperity resembles a waiting for Godot. A more active solution for them is to move to the city, often in the south, in hope for better jobs and life. In today's China, this "better" is generally predicated on joining the capitalist system first as part of the productive labor force, and second, in the urban settings, subscribing to the desires of consumption.

When being plunged into the desiring machine of consumption through sweated labor, migrant workers often get trapped into a highly demanding labor regime, a regime that "turn[s] a young and rural body into an industrialized and productive laborer" (Pun 2005: 77), regulated by imposed timetables and the speed of the assembly line. Sun

Wanning quotes from her interview with a young factory worker from Hunan, who articulates his dream for the future (2012: 76):

> I would like to end my situation as a *dagong* man. I would like to get married, have children, and start my own family. I wish that my life is not controlled by someone else. I would like to be able to say "no" when I don't want to work extra shifts. I don't dream of having lots of money, but it would be good to have some money so that I can do things which I would like to do, rather than being at someone else's disposal.

A statement that expresses both hope and a fear of being left out, this undercurrent of despair surfaces in many accounts of migrant lives. The term *dagong* man or "worker" in the eyes of both public and the workers has evolved into a pejorative term, which significantly deviates from the nobler proletariat under the communist context. Working class, therefore, is the lowest level of social class. In reality, youth, if capable, would generally avoid being labeled as workers. We actually heard from parents compelling their kids to work hard or else they would be factory *dagong* workers. In cities, in general educated youth refuse to work as laborers. In 2007, a survey interestingly found out that only 0.1 percent of Shanghai youngsters claim that they would be willing to be workers (Li 2007). On the levels of discrimination (Gui et al. 2012: 608), they are believed to be of lower quality – *suzhi* – when compared to urbanites. In the words of Ann Anagnost (2004: 190), "the discourse of *suzhi* appears most elaborated in relation to two figures: the body of the rural migrant, which exemplifies *suzhi* in its apparent absence, and the body of the urban, middle-class only child, which is fetishized as a site for the accumulation of the very dimensions of *suzhi* wanting in its 'other.'" The pairing of the single child, who bears the burden of becoming the carrier of *suzhi*, and the migrant worker as its opposite, is provocative, and underlines how China's progress is intimately entangled with the lives of people that are generally rendered invisible. Quite directly so during the Beijing Olympics, when the migrant workers who had done the hard work of building the Olympic city at such an amazing speed had to depart from the city during the games as their presence would symbolize poverty as opposed to the glory and extravagance of Beijing as the host of the Olympics and would be "harmful" to the image of China.

According to Anagnost (2004: 193), *suzhi* "works ideologically as a regime of representation through which subjects recognize their positions within the larger social order." One of the ways to locate the cultural position of these youth workers, as suggested by Sun (2009: 30), is to extend the *suzhi* debate into the realm of popular culture and critically examine their representation. This inspires her to analyze television series that feature migrant workers, and read television as part of a public culture that helps produce a desirable citizen (see Rofel 2007). With the same logic and intention, this chapter articulates the link between media and migrant youth, in which we take the latter not only as media consumers but also as media producers, aside from studying the ways in which they are represented in cinema and popular culture.

While we aim to question any uncritical celebration of China's global rise, similar to the other chapters, we still aim to steer away from presenting only a gloomy picture. While the analysis by Chen and Pun points at grave injustices taking place in China today, we want to avoid articulating only this dark side, to read migrant work only in terms of abuse and hardship. Again, we will walk the tightrope between probing into the hardships and difficulties these youngsters face and their ways of coping and survival. Furthermore, we would like to question the erasure of youth in representations and studies of migrant youth. There, it is generally the issue of labor, rather than being young, that is foregrounded.

We will first engage with the role of the media and popular culture in relation to the lives of migrant youth and engage with representations of migrant youth. As can be seen, most of these representations, in China and overseas, do address the problem of migrant youth as vicious cycles with only symbolic resistance, usually in the form of suicide. Second, we reveal more recent cases that show how social media enable young migrants to become media producers to at least challenge the unjust conditions and critique factories that exploit workers to sustain the state economy of China. Last, we examine cases in which migrant youth use various means, such as new media communication technologies, gaming, and alternative migration patterns, to find pleasure and negotiate their own way of life. While we are aware of cases of miserable, docile migrant youth who are monitored and managed the whole time, we aim to highlight an emerging migrant youth culture that uses the media technologies available to them in new and unexpected ways.

MIGRANT YOUTH, REPRESENTATION, AND DESIRE

The worker has long been an important trope in communist propaganda, just as the countryside was privileged over the urban. In post-1978 China this has tilted radically: "the countryside – once exulted as a sanctuary of enlightenment for urban youth – has become the despised antithesis of modernity" (Y. Wang 2015: 163). Young villagers inhabit a wasteland, the future lies elsewhere, in the city. But in this elsewhere – the city – migrant workers are treated as second rate citizens, they are refused a *hukou*, and thereby the right to the city, and suffer from discrimination in everyday life. In global media, images dominate of factory girls that work endless hours under horrible circumstances that drive them to suicide. The Chinese authorities try to adjust that image in an effort to give a positive image of the migrant worker. Again, the trope of labor by and large rules over youthfulness, as we already observed earlier.

When reviewing the literature, surprisingly little has been published on the role media play in the everyday lives of youth migrant workers. The predominance of the issue of labor is understandable, but also deprives migrant workers of their agency, fun, and pleasure. When media uses are studied, it is often in connection to issues of labor. For example, a study by Daniela Stockmann and Mary Gallagher (2011) is based on a unique survey that includes migrant workers, a population that is generally left out in surveys, as they do not fall under the household registration system. The study shows how media are mobilized to present an idealized picture of labor regulations in China. In line with our argument that the marketization of China's media goes hand in hand with the consolidation of political power, their study shows that workers, after watching a legal show on television, "remained fairly susceptible to positive messages about the labour law" (Stockmann and Gallagher 2011: 453).

Sun analyzes how in an official CCTV series like *Talking about Migrant Workers* (*Huashuo nongmin gong*) from 2009, both tone and script are authoritative and hegemonic, carefully edited and scripted so as to present little ambiguity and sustain the harmony of the country. She quotes the overriding message of the series:

> Glory to rural migrant workers! The contribution you have made to socialist construction is now fully acknowledged by the Chinese people. Pride to rural migrant workers! The efforts you have made to make China a strong nation have captured the imagination of the entire world. (Sun 2013: 6)

In general, the images of migrants tend to be overtly positive and one-sided in these government-related productions. Yet, the migrant workers themselves are there to be seen, rather than heard, as they are not given a voice. This makes Sun conclude that the official documentaries adopt "a politics of recognition that manifests in giving visibility without legitimacy, rhetorical recognition without economic and political substance. These programmes betray a profound anxiety and fear of the prospect of class-based collective consciousness and antagonism" (Sun 2013: 8). But she also shows how other documentaries explore different routes, in which the makers steer away from an authoritative voiceover. A documentary like *Construction Site* (*Gong Di*, Wang Yiqun, 2004) was, for example, successful both inside the system as well as internationally given the "synergy the film has struck between the 'economy of vision' and the 'politics of recognition'" (Sun 2013: 10). Sun points out that the more alternative filmic representations of migrant workers interestingly often come from directors who used to work for CCTV. As such, the state television helps create different voices. What these films and documentaries share, in our view, is that the issues of age and generation are downplayed in favor of the issues of migration and labor.

China's acclaimed filmmaker Jia Zhangke's *A Touch of Sin* from 2013 is one key example of a cinematic representation of migrant workers. In fact, the whole oeuvre of Jia presents a lasting engagement with the fate of migrant workers as well as the places that they leave behind in search of a better life. *A Touch of Sin* consists of four different stories, all of which resemble real events from China's recent past. The story of the Foxconn suicides constitutes one of the backdrops of the movie, which concerns the tale of Xiaohui, who moved to Shenzhen and goes from one discouraging job to the next, struggling with love, life, and work. Enchanted by the prospect of becoming a consumer, as analyzed eloquently by Pun Ngai (2003), he starts working in a night-club where he is confronted with the conspicuous wealth of China's new rich. He falls in love with Lianrong, a girl who works in the same nightclub. In one scene, while they have a break, she checks her iPad, and reads about an official who has been found with 130 Louis Vuitton bags – another sign of the world of consumption they are surrounded with but that will forever remain out of their reach. He declares his love for her, but she replies that in her world, love does not exist, and he hardly knows her. She tells him she already has a three-year-old son, and when he witnesses her giving sexual service to a client, he moves on to another job.

Money drives the people as well the plot forward, even his own family keeps on asking when he will send back some money, a request that drives him to his ultimate deed of committing suicide by jumping out of the window. As Y. Wang writes (2015: 164), "with no money, future, hope or love, Xiaohui is reduced to a bare laborer whose human worth derives exclusively from his production of surplus value. As Xiaohui is disabused of these fantasies, neoliberal logic implodes from within." Hence, he commits suicide. However desperate, his gesture is also an act of resistance, albeit a pessimistic one and only an escape. The movie achieves the unpacking of the inner life of these migrant youth: they are not just victims devoid of agency. Instead, their rich inner lives, which are a complex of love, fear, and desire, are all exposed to the public. While *A Touch of Sin* explores the violence imposed on people by the larger discourses that sustain those in power in China – the state, the businessmen, the local officials – migrant youth hold the power to take up a mischievous role and fight back, symbolically or literally. They are modern knights, using their *wuxia* skills to fight the violence of the system. Sometimes quite literally so: one character in the movie, working in a beauty parlor, uses her fighting skills to kill an abusive customer – in the scene, Jia clearly mobilizes a *wuxia* aesthetics.

While state media present an all too glamorous image of migrant workers, representations in global media also run the danger of presenting an almost equally one-sided flip side. *Last Train Home* (2009) is an internationally award-winning documentary in film festivals in Montreal and Amsterdam, and is a Canadian and Chinese co-production, financed by foreign funding bodies. The director Fan Lixin tells the story of the Zhang family who moved from rural

Sichuan to Guangdong province for work. The camera follows the lives of middle-aged father Zhang Changhua and his wife Chen Suqing, who went back home during the Spring Festival and soon sparked off an incident about why their 16-year-old daughter Zhang Qin desired to follow in their footsteps, escape the village, and try her luck further down south. What is revealing in this film is how the character Qin eventually becomes a young migrant worker. She illustrates how the migration and labor problem evolves into a generational conflict with the parents.

When migrant workers have children, they are faced with a difficult choice: do they leave them behind, or do they bring them to the city where they work? It is estimated that in 2013, there were around 61 million "left-behind children" with 42.8 percent of them having both of their parents working as migrant workers in the city (Xinhua 2013). In the movie, the relationship between the two "left-behind" children and their parents becomes full of tension and conflicts. The grandmother takes care of the children and attempts to maintain the status quo, continually reiterating the importance of Confucian filial piety and academic achievement – the two domains that we emphasized in chapter 1 that sustain the system. The story starts with an internal struggle of the mother to buy a train ticket to return home. The latter triggered the desire of the daughter to cease schooling and follow her parents, in particular, when she was given a mobile phone. The key point here is that the migrant status of their parents actually passed on a desire to their child, thus perpetuating the rural-to-city migration line. The irregularity here is that at this juncture, two of the pillars of the cultural firewall, familism and a state-supported pedagogy, are being challenged by the rapidly growing inequality between the countryside and the city. A growing desire to become part of a market economy and to consume thus undermines both the family and education. Eventually Qin drops out of school, she ends up being a young worker in a clothes factory, lined up alongside many other workers. Yet, she still expresses being unhappy there, without family, and then proclaims her freedom by shopping with her friends. It is the desiring machine called consumption that justifies her continuous work as a migrant worker in conjunction with the solitude of the city and the lack of prospects in the countryside. At the end of the movie, we see Qin working in a nightclub where she believes she earns more. In the world of abundance and conspicuous consumption, we see her serving the new rich of China. She claims to "pursue her dreams," but their fulfillment seems highly unlikely; instead, she indeed seems to repeat the life of her parents. Without improvements to the system, the cycle of desire and migration is likely to be repeated from one generation to the next.

We do not wish to claim that such a documentary is a real and truthful representation of the life of youth migrant workers. We see mediations like a documentary as a double refraction: it is a mediation through the camera, of a refraction, caused by the point of view – or habitus – of the filmmaker and his team, of reality (see Shohat and Stam 1994). This is why it is dangerous to conflate a representation of reality with reality itself – both are mutually constitutive, reality produces representations that impact on reality.

One refraction we can witness in *Last Train Home* is the cinematic juxtaposition between the countryside and the city, a binary framework that keeps on haunting the representation of migrant workers, in which the lush, green countryside is juxtaposed to the grey city. It romantically inverts the idealization of the city as the locus of modernity; it now validates nature as the place of innocence and joy, and the city as the place of contamination and unhappiness. This ideological juxtaposition flattens out complexities, romanticizing the countryside at the expense of city life. This feeds into a quite stereotypical depiction of the marginalization of migrant workers whose lives seem to have no hope. However, what we want to present with our ethnographic data is that, despite the miserable life and the vicious cycle of the youth migrant workers, with new resources and technologies, there are new youth spaces being carved out.

MIGRANT YOUTH AS MEDIA PRODUCERS

The discourse of marginalization of youth is increasingly supplemented by discourses of migrant youth who are more expressive in articulating their lives and resistance on social media and the Internet. Described in Qiu et al.'s study (2009: 120) is a young female migrant worker, Han Ying, who at the age of 16 left home in rural Sichuan to work in Chengdu, where she worked as a waitress, hairdresser, construction worker, and street cleaner, among other jobs. She started blogging in 2006 and by 2008 her blog had attracted a million visits. Her short writings, illustrated with numerous photographs, reveal personal emotions ranging from homesickness, childhood memories, and her aspirations for the future (Qiu et al. 2009). By 2015, her blog has ceased to exist, attesting to the ephemeral nature of digital environments. But in her wake, numerous migrant workers have started to become media producers. With the ready availability of digital platforms, it has become increasingly easy for migrant youth to produce media content themselves. Websites, blogs, *Weixin* (Wechat) groups, and *Weibo* postings are used to share poetry, novels, short clips, songs, pictures, diaries and the like. Each platform comes with its own specific affordances and constraints; each has its own particular logic and political economy, making it problematic to write of "digital technologies" or "the Internet" as if it were a singular monolithic entity. For example, whereas *Weibo* is a public platform, *Weixin* (or Wechat) is more private; it facilitates privately shared social networks similar to Facebook groups. Taken together, however, these different technologies do allow young migrant workers to express their own voice, as well as to mobilize themselves. In the context of this chapter, we are more concerned with the media contents they produce, rather than with the political ramifications of mobilization of migrant workers through social media (for that, see Yang 2011).

Sun explores how the poetry of migrant workers articulates a subaltern imagination (2010). She analyzes three recurring tropes in migrant poetry: "alienation of the body in the industrial regime, displacement and homesickness, and disenchantment with the south" (2010: 296). As with other analyses, the theme of labor overrides the theme of youth, and when they do intersect, it is labor abuse that receives most attention. For example, in her reference to an old incident in 1998 when a migrant worker, 23-year-old Liu Huangqi, passed out and died after working several extra shifts, his sister Luo Deyuan dedicated a poem to him, titled "Liu Huangqi, my *dagong* brother" (Sun 2010: 298):

Your digestive system is bleeding
Your respiratory system has just collapsed
Your life is near its end
Yet you still want to punch your card
"They will fine me if I am late," you said
My brother, why were you so scared?
We are not indentured labourers
Nor are we modern slaves
Why can't we simply say "no"
And raise our indignant fists!

What these poems do is articulate a counter-hegemonic perspective that refuses to accept the system and structure; they circulate online and survive outside the realm and control of the state-owned media. Words like these, that continue to be posted online, undermine the hegemonic discourse of harmony as well as Xi Jinping's "China Dream." They render the pain of migrant labor visible in a system that is at pains to keep this invisible.

Chan (2002) studied the letters of migrant workers that are sent to relatives and close friends in a time without social media. The main themes she traced were related to wages, finding a job, working overtime, physical existence, and loneliness. Chan explains that "the young people had to confront factory life on their own. Letters became an important part of their lives: they were important sources of information about job opportunities and, more importantly, their only meaningful contact with the world beyond the factory and dormitory walls" (Chan 2002: 176). She explains how, "as revealed in these letters, workers become consumed by the most primary concerns – a subsistence income, food, and health....Leisure and entertainment are not part of their lives" (2002: 182). What is different today when compared to Chan's study is not only the availability of entertainment for workers through different media, but also the ease with which the personal can be turned into a public statement. When shared on their Wechat moments, the images, testimonies, poems, and complaints of migrant workers can soon go viral. The personal and private can thus be turned into a more public event – a virtual equivalent of the public privacy we witness in the parks with lovers kissing in the dark.

These individual efforts are now supported and sustained by the work of many NGOs and worker concern groups in China, Taiwan, and Hong Kong. In June 2015, a naked female demonstrator from a Taiwan NGO, namely Worker's Solidarity, went to the headquarters of Hon Hai Precision Industry that runs China's Foxconn to protest against the industry's exploitation of workers in China (Yang 2015). It was a flash mob strategy that encountered resistance from security guards at the shopping mall, and soon became a media event that attracted enough attention from social media to report the cases of three workers who worked in Foxconn as factory workers and were suffering from leukemia. Two of them died while the third, Yang Dan, still survived but had to pay huge medical bills to extend her life.

Yang Dan was a young lady who started working for the company at the age of 19. She was part of the assembly line for testing and assembling mobile phones in the Foxconn plant in Shenzhen. In the social media report, Dan said

> Basically every day in every assembly room, [I had to] walk through the radiation from thousands of mobile phone products, and all mobile phones were in switched-on mode, and in the room, thousands of computers were switched on. [I] was simultaneously exposed to many scanners, and radiation. (Yang 2015)

She then explained vividly how she failed to notice the radiation in the beginning, but then developed symptoms, and was hospitalized and informed of the disease. She received chemotherapy to slow down the process of deterioration. Quite obviously, these cases are not reported in China because they are not "harmonious" to the society and will therefore be banned, from *Weibo* to state media. Even in Taiwan, it was said that these reports were rarely featured in mass media because the powerful corporations tend to threaten to sue reporters for libel. But before such bans, social media are used by the migrant youth and their family members to distribute their own writings and messages, which otherwise would never be seen by the public. The messages will thus continue to circulate. Whereas the character in *A Touch of Sin* resisted by way of suicide, youth described here are more concerted, proactive, and insightful enough to disseminate their counter-statement against the dominant voices of the corporations. An open letter posted in conjunction with a social media report entitled "A Letter to Foxconn Apple Company," concluded with (Civil Media Taiwan 2015):

> What makes one infuriated is that Foxconn said Yang Dan is not their employee; [she] cannot confirm it is an occupational disease. We couldn't accept this; we put the case to court. Now the court

acknowledged Yang Dan's worker relationship. [Thus we] can proceed with occupational medical examination. But half a year was gone. For a patient, what will she have gone through in such half a year? Our leaders, you can think about that. [We] hope the leaders of Foxconn see our pains so that you can work with us, [and] give us a satisfied result. We are waiting for money to save a life. Wish good guys a healthy life…A person who is waiting for money to save a life.

Yang Min. June 15, 2015

The essence of this letter is a direct demand for the company to respond. With social media, and its transnational nature, the Taiwan site not only recognizes and legitimizes the rights of the youth migrant workers and their relatives but also provides additional cultural spaces for this youth to voice their demands. In the letter, it is noticed that youth no longer blame the system or society for its indifference. Rather it begs the existing controlling system, in this case the Chinese court, for legitimation. Migrant youth regain here their individual identity, they move beyond the image of being merely ordinary cogs in the factory machine.

MIGRANT YOUTH AND NEW MEDIA TECHNOLOGIES

We witness an important disjuncture here between mass media like television and digital media, with the latter being more difficult to control, more interactive, and allowing for the establishment of inter-personal networks over time and space. One could lament that digital communication technologies have become extra limbs for the employer to command closer control and surveillance. For example, it is now quite common that the factory management controls the use of mobile devices among migrant factory workers. Female workers are often not allowed to bring their mobile phones into the factory (Qiu et al. 2009:

188). Even more so, companies build concentrated collective networks and distribute phones among workers, the fancy ones to high ranked managers: "this wireless phone system extends control over employees, who are required to keep the phone on wherever they go so that upper-level managers can reach their subordinates immediately" (Qiu et al. 2009: 190).

But still, while mass media seem to be by and large tools to sustain the political status quo in China, it is digital media in various forms that help young Chinese migrant workers to imagine and aspire to life differently. Yet, these are simultaneously the tools used by both factories and the state to govern them; as such there is no reason for any techno-optimism or to read these tools as intrinsically liberating or enabling – as we also discussed in chapter 2. Their affordances are prescribed by the specific technological socio-political constellation of China, and since only a few technology-savvy youngsters know how to circumvent the firewall through the use of VPN accounts – an alternative that usually comes with a price that is out of reach for migrant workers – the potential of the Internet to change the lives and fate of migrant workers remains curtailed.

After their long working hours that often run from 9 to 9, young migrant workers quickly dash back to their dormitory to connect to the Internet again on their mobile phones. Media technologies offer them ways to not only escape from their everyday chores, but also reconnect with their hometown. One's hometown is important, because after migration, people connect with others and find jobs through relationships with people from their hometown. Also here, mobile phone technologies are of pivotal importance. As Qiu et al. argue,

Working-class ICTs are not just gadgets; they also serve as a set of social, cultural, and political conditions running through migrant populations. ICT connectivity may empower migrants in pursuit of personal objectives. But it may also subject them to new systems of control, exploitation, and alienation and other ways of disempowerment by service providers, employers, or state actors, at work or at home. (2009: 86)

New communication technologies help connect migrant youth with their surroundings, the rural, their hometowns, and the world. In her book-length study on migrants and mobile phones, Cara Wallis (2013: 4) probes into "how social constructions of gender-, class-, age-, and place-based identities produce particular engagements with mobile technologies, which in turn reproduce and restructure these identities." Mobile phones can create new forms of community, she shows, but also produce exclusions, for example when the employer confiscates the phones during working time. Wallis coins the term "immobile mobility" to characterize the uses of the mobile phone. It points to the fact that mobile phones are often used from the same location, by people whose lives are highly repetitive, and deeply constrained by the workplace and dormitory rules. The mobile phone offers a way out, albeit temporal, but it may also reify the marginalization of migrant women. As such, immobile mobilization "can be liberating and constraining, creating new opportunities for empowerment and disempowerment" (Wallis 2013: 7). Her argument is in line with our contention that youth culture in China is characterized by the constant oscillation between control and being controlled, between technologies of the self and technologies of subjection. In the case of migrant youth, these dynamics are played out even more strongly, given the multiple ways in which they are haunted by stigmatization and stereotypes. One other way to negotiate this tension is through computer gaming.

GAMING AND IMMATERIAL LABOR

In China, the sight of young workers lingering in Internet cafés is common. Our experience and observation in Internet cafés is quite astonishing. In 2010, a Beijing local student guided us to an Internet café in Haidian District, where many important universities and high schools cluster. One of us was shown along a few narrow lanes or *hutong*, completely losing our sense of direction, until we saw a PC sign outside a half-painted door. We went inside and it was a completely undecorated white room, nothing of it even remotely resembled a "café." We were attracted by a number of computers with old monitors being used by young people who had paid. To avoid disrupting the atmosphere, we lowered our voices and talked to those gamers who were obviously busy gaming. With the almost implicit consent of the manager of the small PC café, we could only briefly ask a few questions to male youngsters sitting nearby. The gamers never gave full answers to consecutive questions and we remember only a few keywords mentioned. Roughly, the young worker who seemed to work as a low-level service or *dagong* worker in Beijing said that there was nothing meaningful to do in life or in his job. He had no family or friends in Beijing, so lingering in the virtual world by playing computer games is the most economic way. It is not just that gaming is a way of passing the leisure time. He interacts with virtual friends using Tencent's QQ public chat room that ties in with the game. In addition, he created private and group QQ chat rooms with his "clan," which extends his network of friends to other workers or non-workers, with whom he can share his views in a realm outside the factory. Above all, the communication platform, part of the quite unique game world, imbued the migrant worker with a strong sense of achievement when he succeeded in raising the level of his avatar by accomplishing the game mission (e.g. *yunbiao*, or protection of carts full of treasure while the avatar moves from one place to another). He celebrated the triumphant moment of combat with other gamers in the massive multiple-player online game (MMORPG). Among the many games he played was Zhengtu, literally meaning adventure, which was the most popular online game in China. As of 2008 its number of concurrent users amounted to 300,000 on average and reached a peak of 2,000,000.

Later we attempted to understand why migrant youth are so passionate about Zhengtu by interviewing the Shanghai-based game company Giant Interactive Group, game guilds, and other gamers. Apparently, migrant workers were attracted by Zhengtu's "forever free" slogan, which significantly lowers the minimum threshold of the game. In the game, what makes the impossible possible is the combat between the migrant workers and players with a well-off background, thus turning the struggle into a symbolic one between the haves and the have-nots, and between the wealthy and the poor. This all takes place in the fictive cities of the game: the Royal City and the Phoenix City. Mimicking the real world, well-off game players can often pay to achieve what they want to accomplish in the game world; by exchanging their real RMB for gold coins, rich gamers can easily buy off their level and time for accumulating levels of experience, and acquire more virtual tools for different purposes. However, migrant workers compensate for their lack of resources with their available time, which is comparatively more. The work of this migrant laborer here is equivalent to immaterial labor (Lazzarato 1996), a type of labor that is expressed in time rather than the actual labor and production in the factory. This time is spent in the game for their avatar to accumulate their five traits, namely power, intellectual ability, swiftness, spirituality, and physical strength. At this juncture, the game world can be understood as the very first and perhaps the only equal-and-same platform that migrant workers can use together with, and compete with, urban youth dwellers. That explains why the migrant workers that we talked to at the Internet café are willing to spend long hours there: they derive their pleasure by creating their own possibility of beating their superior with their actual labor in Zhengtu, an ahistorical and re-invented Chinese world of 10 kingdoms where they have a chance to outperform their more affluent competitors, although in practice the resource-rich player can readily gain an upper hand.

The role of the state in maintaining fair play in the online game is most celebrated by gamers. Without going deeper into the political economy of the gaming industries, we would like to convey the idea of how the state has intervened more than once at different stages to halt the strategy of the game companies reaping unreasonable profits. Zhengtu once charged players RMB1 to acquire a virtual key to unlock a box of big treasure basically making every gamer pay if they want to continue to proceed with level elevation. Such a strategy was soon copied by other game companies for other online games. Obviously the loser was the resource-poor gamers who could not afford to pay in the long run. No sooner had gamers campaigned against the charge than the Ministry of Culture and Ministry of Commerce jointly inaugurated the "Notice about Management over Trading of Virtual Currency of Online Game Industry," which represented a quick response to gamers' grievances about gaming companies ripping them off, resulting in the cancellation of the virtual key charges. This was a virtual-and-yet-real online movement. The gamers counted on the state's regulatory power to bring back the game world to a virtual ideal. This is coherent with our earlier argument that the youth nowadays do not deliberately topple the system but revert back to the rule of state authority to support their causes.

In this sense, youth's "resistance," understood in the gaming context of the migrant youth, neither modifies forcefully the socioeconomic conditions in which they reside nor reverses the class relationship with Foxconn or other factory owners. They seek their own pleasure in the cultural arena and focus on small joys they experience in a fair game contest from player-killing (PK) to *wulin* or public championship and national warfare. After our interactions with the gamers, we always have the impression that gamers, in particular the have-nots, are committed to the ideals of the game world – autonomy, fairness, and merit-based equality. Coincidently, the game comes from one of China's biggest game companies named PerfectWorld. This world is, of course, not perfect, but it is interesting to see how some form of self-regulation does exist. When Zhengtu was first launched, the game world was a pseudo-capitalist world: migrant workers could gain silver coins by selling their immaterial labor, but gold coins were only available for those who pay. There were also rules limiting certain activities such as immigration and marriage between avatars, both of which require gold coins. Resource-poor gamers started to complain, and with other semi-state efforts – such as the Chinese Youth's Internet Association's green game campaign to dilute its connotation of gambling – in August 2006, Zhengtu started to release "salary" in the form of gold coins to those gamers above level 60, gaming over 60 hours monthly and those who attain a certain level of fame or honor. In this sense, migrant gamers at least feel empowered that they can defend a cultural world, though capitalist-driven, with their labor.

GOLDFARMING VERSUS FARMING

Going back to our observation in the Internet café, we actually did not stay long every time. Given the nature of the dual immaterial labor and migrant labor of these workers, one can presume that they have no great interest in talking to us. We have no role in advancing either their rights in the factory or rights in the virtual world. In the particular observation that we mentioned, before leaving, we tried to get the contact details of the young worker. He refused saying only that probably we would not meet again because he had to go back to his village if there was "no achievement," and apparently he did not expect there to be any achievement for him thereafter.

Young migrant workers have to swallow long and boring work hours – a sentiment that is shared by all studies among migrant labor – and communication technologies or gaming are ways for youth to escape or negotiate an alternative, more aspiring subjectivity. However, when they grow older, marriage and having children slowly become more pressing issues. At this point, familism is at work again, and they may just go back home and forget the city dream. When some migrant youth who are gamers go back to their villages, the only residual value is not the money they have saved, but the skills and techniques in gaming. Then they may transform this skill into labor, essentially folding their docile body back into the political economy of the industry, by again, working 9 to 9, or even longer and overnight, to serve clients in the first world and rich players from big cities in China, to develop and train their avatars, and "exercise" them when the clients are too busy. These are called "goldfarmers." Goldfarming is a quite extreme example of the outsourcing of labor on a global and national scale, bringing to mind also the call centers in India and other developing countries. In our case, China is also illustrative of the digital sweatshop of a global gaming world. As seen in our examples, it is also common for migrant youth workers to go back to their hometowns in rural, second or third tier cities to start their second career – from a factory worker to a global-factory-game worker.

In the 2006 documentary *Cyber Coolies*, Dutch documentary maker Floris-Jan van Luyn gave a detailed account of the lives of migrant youth in Zhengzhou. These goldfarmers started working in Internet cafés as professional gamers, working mostly for Western gamers in dull repetitive digital labor that is required to bring the player in the game World of Warcraft to a higher level. The documentary follows Jing and Feng in their work as goldfarmers with images of them interlaced with shots from the game, turning them visually into *kungfu* masters and strong and sexy heroines respectively. The contrast with the bleak emotionless expression on their faces underlines the repetitiveness of their work and stresses the difference between online and offline realities. Jing, a young female goldfarmer who explains she wanted to escape the surveillance of her parents in her move to Shanghai, tells how her boss is pushing her to work hard in this job:

> My boss told me I really have to finish this job tonight. The client wants to get a certain amount of ore, but I am not there yet. I am afraid I won't manage.

These professional gamers work more than ten hours a day, and usually stay for less than a year in this job. The metaphorical implications of the job are uncanny; they attest not only to the globalization of labor – by now, even those who stay put in their villages are implicated in a global labor regime – the documentary also shows how this globalization of labor remains entrenched in strong inequalities of power. Young workers may work less in the mines today – although they still do – the new modes of labor resemble work in the shafts, albeit in a digital shaft, with digital ore. But the informants also express a sense of empowerment. For example Dong, a young girl, explains, drawing on a strong binary between the real and the virtual:

> I feel stronger and more successful in this virtual world, when I am tired and someone tries to do a PK – a player kill – on me, and I still manage to win, then I am really super happy. This is success in the virtual world, I don't experience that in the real world. In the real world, as a girl, you can't start fighting that easily.…The virtual world has much less restrictions, is more free. That is what I am looking for: freedom.

While in academic discourse the binary between the real and the virtual has been rightly contested (Hine 2015), in the everyday life of Dong we can still trace its clear articulation, the virtual provides an escape from the real, it empowers her and gives pleasure, but also prompts her to be aware of the limitations and lack of freedom she experiences in the real world.

In one scene the film creates a graphic match between the virtual and the real world. We see how Wang is playing a character in World of Warcraft that flies on a bird, the bird flies over the mountains to the countryside. There the virtual morphs into the real, and we see how Wang returns to his family in his hometown. The contrast between the virtual world and his life in the city of Zhengzhou and his background in a small rural village cannot be bigger, and symbolizes the fast pace of change in China. With a poster of Chairman Mao still hanging on his wall, we hear his father explain:

> He is grown up now, able to take care of himself, I hope he will become rich. I hope he will marry, obeys the law, I hope he will be very successful and act according to the law.

The prominence of wealth, success and obeying the law resonate with our analysis in chapter 1 on the power of the forces of family, school, and state. His father is unable to explain what kind of job his son does, "something like selling computers," he says. Wang explains that he plays computer games for his boss in an Internet café, but his father does not understand what computer games are. Ostensibly the scene is illustrative of the generation gap, especially between migrant youth workers and their parents, when the latter stay in the countryside. Yet, from the perspective of the young boy, life may not be as miserable as we described. The game world also empowers the gamer, and to read them purely as victims of a global game labor regime would deny him or her his own agency, pleasure, and creativity derived from gaming. Goldfarmers' "digital work" is preferred above working unremittingly on tormenting jobs in a factory or uninspiring chores on farms.

What, then, is driving the life of the young migrant who returns home? He capitalizes on his gaming skills, making his immaterial labor valuable and not easily replaceable. At the same time, his voluntary practice to continue to support his family financially by working hard demonstrates that he is filial and obedient to his parents. It is what Foucault called "techniques of the self" or arts of existence that the youth mobilize to (re)adapt to the new environment and to find a way where their family can understand their life and work. Gaming skills are used as a way to transform themselves and shape their own values and aesthetics (Foucault 1990: 10–11). Such techniques of the self, however, cannot be fulfilled without the techniques of the digital world he practiced everyday during the leisure time while he was still a migrant worker – both are mutually constitutive.

We interviewed a start-up gaming company in 2011 in Beijing when online gaming was in its heyday in China (Fung forthcoming). The young boss of the company was a friend of ours. He and his business partner simply rented an office just adjacent to the high-tech *Zhong-guancun* Science Park area, no more than a simple office lacking any decorations, with computers for game development. Living on a low stipend, they ran this risky business with an angel fund injected into the company, aiming to develop an online strategic game, one that is simple enough like playing chess. Yet, for an online game like that, the business still needed to hire a team of four additional paid staff. These four employees hardly responded to us during our visit to the company and our play with the beta version of the game. But then later we heard from the owner that among the team, apart from university graduates, some are high school graduates with strong techniques in gaming and game programming. Before they were recruited, they worked on some goldfarming jobs to sustain their living. Of course, now, because of their acquired skills, they have been able to transform themselves into a full-time staff member in a formal gaming company in the heart of Beijing. The techniques of the game world, together with their passion for games, have increased their life choices, mobility, and cultural life in the city; now they did not need to go back to their hometowns to work as farmers or goldfarmers.

FROM VILLAGE TO ART VILLAGE: NEW SPACES AND MOBILITY

Today migrant workers are increasingly capable of moving to new spaces where the conditions of life may be relatively better. So far we have discussed the immobile mobility of youth due to the accessibility of social media, digital technologies, and techniques for youth workers. Goldfarming is already a move away from working in the factory, but there are other possibilities as well, for example working in an art village.

Just across the border from the cosmopolitan Hong Kong, in Shenzhen there is the Dafen Art Village, an indigenous village of 0.4 square kilometers that hosts 40 sizable oil painting dealers and 1,200 art galleries that employ around 8,000 young migrants from different places in China. Most young artists coming to Dafen acknowledge that they come for a living, not to realize their artistic dreams but to make a living by spending their everyday life unambiguously reproducing famous Western paintings from Vincent van Gogh, Salvador Dali, Pablo Picasso, to name a few, and occasionally some contemporary Chinese masterpieces, most notably, those from Yue Minjun. Since 2000, the Dafen Art Village has been taken shape as a center for oil painting reproduction, sales and distribution, and now the oil painting business also galvanizes other art forms such as calligraphy, embroidery, sculpture, and art crafts as the secondary business in the village. Most ubiquitous art we see in hotels across the world comes from Dafen (Wong 2013).

In the eyes of youth workers, Dafen Art Village can be conceived as the artistic version of China's assembly line factory, only this time the factory fabricates not clothes, toys, iPhones, nor television sets, but replicas of paintings that are destined to be put in the living rooms of a decent household or the lobby of a hotel. Most of these young kids did not graduate from a famous art academy in a big city, so they flock to the village to earn a living. Once there, they develop their skills, which results in a social and professional hierarchy being established in Dafen, with some becoming closer to the notion of "artist" than others, as analyzed in Winnie Wong's *Van Gogh on Demand: China and the Readymade* (2013). She explains how, in the end, painters in Dafen do aspire to become an artist in some way or other. She writes, "Dafen painters might define their success as 'artists' in different ways – some by professional and social stature, some by exhibition and travel opportunities, some by the market value of their works – but their desire to claim that authorial status of 'artist' is consistent and wide-spread" (2013: 218).

However, youth migrants working in Dafen are still subject to harm and poor conditions such as inhaling volatile solvent for oil painting, and working and sleeping, eating and painting in small, shabby village houses that are converted into a dormitory. They work 6 days a week for a measly RMB1,500 a month (for a very junior worker that we talked to). But again, as Wong's study also shows, to frame Dafen only in terms of abuse and assembly line production would do injustice to

Image 6. A painter in Dafen Art Village (photo by Jeroen de Kloet in 2016)

what is actually going on, and would deprive the workers from their agency and, indeed, inspiration and creativity.

Tan Ming is a 25-year-old painter/worker, who finished high school four years before we interviewed him in 2013. He first went to Jiangmen, to work as a customs service worker, making cold calls. He did that for half a year, but then, in high school he learned a bit about making sketches and when he heard of painting apprenticeship possibilities in Shenzhen, he came to Dafen. After three months' training he started working. At first, his work was not good enough to sell and he earned very little money. He borrowed from his family, and painted a lot at a low price. He is not an employee but rents his own place and pays for everything himself. One painting takes half a day to finish, on average. He works practically all of the time, if he has orders. He doesn't know about the future, but he keeps on saying that he is not good enough, both in terms of technique and the fact that what he paints are copies, not original works. Thus, as Wong mentioned in her study, in the end the notions of authorship and becoming an artist do function as important aspiring principles – or obstacles.

Similar to the goldfarmers we discussed previously, young Dafen migrant painters develop and mobilize their skills and techniques to become an "artist" instead of "just" a worker. We casually talked to a few painters lingering on the backstreet of the shops and some owners of galleries. The "artists" did not really chat a lot; they claimed to feel satisfied with their job as an "artist" in the village. The most common reply was that it was "better than in the rural areas." They explained to us it is still very hard work, hence the low number of female painters. Many would start painting just one part of a painting, for example specializing in trees, and slowly move up to copy full paintings. Others also start by copying photographs of clients. Interestingly, according to the bosses we talked to, the economic operations of their work became increasingly difficult to sustain. The increased salary of the skilled youth worker is a pressure on them. Skilled manpower, their availability and their ability to retain them slowly becomes difficult, putting downward pressure on the profits of their work. When we talked to one gallery owner, who explained that his painters made one full work rather than painting only parts, it was interesting to see how he wanted us to avoid connotations of labor only. He prefers to call his employees "painters" (*huajia*) and when we mentioned the term workplace (*gongchang*), he corrected that to "*gongzuoshi*," which means studio.

In October 2012, with a view to retaining skilled youth labor, Longgang District, which governs Dafen, launched the "Management and Implementation Scheme for Longgang District Dafen Art Village Talents' Public Rental," offering existing art workers above 18 years of age working in Dafen Village and their family public housing with a 30–50 percent market discount. More experienced workers are given priority; they could be offered housing with three bedrooms and workers with family are also given a bigger apartment. All these can be seen as government efforts to improve the life of migrant youth in Dafen so that they can continue to sustain the Art Village. The latter is now listed by Longgang District and Shenzhen City as "Model of National Base of Cultural Industry" where numerous top Party leaders have paid visits. Dafen even featured in the Shanghai Expo of 2010 (Wong 2013). Thus, the experiences and skills of these migrant workers are validated officially and publicly, something that rarely happens with other forms of migrant labor.

From have-nots, they have become employees of Shenzhen, enjoying at least equivalent welfare to Shenzhen residents working in offices and other non-laboring jobs. Compared to the migrant workers portrayed in documentary and media, the young migrant workers have changed the discourse from a politics of recognition to a discourse of values, dignity, and self-worth. Besides, early in 2015, Dafen Village announced plans to launch the Cumulus Global Design Academy, which is a design competition jointly organized by Tongji University, a federation of design and media schools, and the Shenzhen government in the second half of the year. In this plan to attract new workers, the promotion of Cumulus includes the slogan "creativity apart from duplication," thus strengthening the discourse of arts in addition to technique and craftsmanship, and above all, the invitation was directed not to painting workers, but to painting masters. It is this prospect for upward mobility of the migrant workers that inspired their move to Dafen. By gesturing to the discourse of true authorship, real artists, and authentic work, this move at the same time feeds into a hegemonic discourse of what constitutes real art, and its underpinning logic of authorship and copyright protection (see Pang 2012). But judging from our ethnographic observations, this move will never be complete, as Dafen also allows for a critical intervention in the workings of the global art world.

One widely reported event about Dafen is their different kinds of painting competitions. These competitions started around May 2006, and there was widespread media coverage of the contest among 110 Dafen artists to see who could paint the best duplication. Recently, these competitions have become more structurally organized by the city and district government. A contest worth mentioning is the second professional competition in May 2004 organized again by different governing units of Dafen Village. There were 100 artists competing for 25 attractive prizes. The most cherished prize is the residential account or *hukou* of Shenzhen. That implies that the government then recognizes the official status of these migrant workers, or at least the more professional and skillful ones. More unexpectedly, the prize was given to a deaf and dumb "artist." This is one example of the workings of governmentality, in which a citizenry is being produced. This is not about top-down control or direct suppression of the subordinated; instead, it is about inspiring workers with hardly any social status to continue to work for the prosperity of the city. From the perspective of the youth rural "artists," their China Dream is to become a real recognized artist in the city, as Wong explained in her study. And local authorities try to accommodate this dream, so as to fold the workers back into the system. But this mode of governance comes with the emergence of new subjectivities: comparatively they may still be quite poor, but they have reworked the rules of the city, taken pleasure in their aspiring pseudo-artist status, and crafted out a cultural artistic space, through the duplication of global artworks.

CONCLUSION

The moment a young person becomes a migrant worker, it seems that the latter label takes over. In other words, mediations of migrant youth stress their status as a migrant and a worker, their bodies become laboring bodies, objectified and then exploited, rather than sites of longing and belonging. As such, they seem to be deprived of their youthfulness. In this chapter, we have revealed media portrayals that expose the exploitation, despondency, and torment of migrant workers in large factories, and ultimately, becoming a slog without freedom, a life devoid of individual being, and a decaying body that moves – deliberately or not – toward death. While such critiques of the labor regime in China are urgent, we have tried to show in this chapter how the lives of migrant youth are more intricate, and can and should not be framed solely in terms of abuse, control, and neglect. We argue that it is dangerous to deprive young migrant workers of their youth, and that it is thus important not to deny their possible hope, options, and search for alternatives. This, however, is not a simple task for all youth in China, given the huge gap between the rich and the poor, between the city and the countryside, and between the haves and the have-nots. In this chapter, we have documented cases in which youth derive pleasure from using mobile phones, create networks, counter exploitation, avail themselves of their bodily skills or techniques, refute the label of worker, and ultimately seek recognition, adapt to urbanity, and develop mobility.

In our analysis of Jia Zhangke's *A Touch of Sin*, we have shown how they transform themselves to contemporary *wuxia* warriors that are always on the move, reclaiming their right to life, to work, and to love. We have shown how migrant youth workers turn into poets, artists, legitimate city citizens, and thereby also reclaim their creativity, dignity, and citizenship. Communication technologies, social media, techniques, skills, imagination, and real labor are youth migrants' resources to extend their cultural practices, liminal space, and autonomy. We do not want to simply celebrate this, the space of possibility depends on many factors, including regulations, social constraints, luck, and fate. Our analysis widens the inquiry not only toward the possibility for different depictions of migrant youth in media and in daily life; we also argue for more attention to the products – such as the game world, avatars and artworks as illustrated in this chapter – that are produced by themselves. In sum, we present a modest attempt, echoing with other chapters, to show that governmentality, biopolitics, and technologies of the self are mutually constitutive. There is opposition amidst subordination, optimism following domination, and mobility behind relegation. These are hopeful and promising strategies, we argue, that help to counter discourses that portray them either in terms of heroic martyr, or as pure victims of a global neoliberal regime. The challenge for future analyses remains how to dissect moments between the forces of manipulation, despair, and destitution, and the possibilities of hope and aspiration.

Conclusion: Youth and Hope ────────────

Youth has to experience different challenges. Only by taking part in practice [can the young people] be toughened and hardened into steel; [they] grow in storm. This is exactly the reason. Hoping not to overcome difficulties [and] obstacles, and to grow easily, this would not increase wisdom.

Guo Moruo (1892–1978)

It seems that in China, the path of youth is not easy, nor is it supposed to be. Guo Moruo is an important poet and the purported founder of modern Chinese poetry, a literary movement associated with progressive New Culture and the May Fourth Movement in 1919. Despite his reformist mind-set, together with his effort to advance the peace movement and scientific development in China, his opinion on youth seems less revolutionary or progressive. This may be connected to his precarious life during the Cultural Revolution, in which he had to declare that his own work should be burned. In the throes of a life-threatening movement, or in a restraining social environment nowadays, youth are expected to abide by the rules, strive against inequality, and take extra efforts to survive and excel.

In this book we have built upon our experiences in China over the past years to explore youth's online activities, fandom, migrant labor, gendered disputes, goldfarming and gaming, and media consumption practices, to name but a few, that we have used as a prism to describe the rich, vibrant, and diverse youth cultures of China. In different chapters we have highlighted the available resources that they could build on to carve out their own space in a rapidly globalizing and urbanizing China, ranging from global culture, online fandom practices that bear the promise of freedom and pleasure, unfailing networked support through social media, to the very specific skills and techniques that they acquire with the uninterrupted passion of gaming. These cultural resources and their variations have extended the options, possibilities, and alternatives that youth could create, resulting in various forms of visible youth cultures. At the same time, we have shown how these same resources are part and parcel of the intensification of power, also how these domains are entangled with the regimes of the state, the family, and the school or workplace. Rather than reading them as intrinsically liberating or emancipatory forces, we have analyzed this complex entanglement, and pointed at how there may at most be *moments* at specific *places* – offline or online – in which alternative subjectivities will be articulated.

In studying youth, we are committed to an ethnographic approach in which we take seriously their own experiences, thoughts, hopes, and aspirations, rather than relying on the multiple discourses that proliferate around youth – be they from educators, politicians, academics, or journalists. Thus, in addition to the textual approaches centering on mediated expressions of youth in, among others, cinema, music, and poetry, that we have used in this book, we have drawn on ethnographic studies from others and, mostly, ourselves. Furthermore, it is our contention that through the consumption of such cultural materials, youth spaces and subjectivities are produced (Eglinton 2012). Even state propaganda allows for a critical reading at times, as youth like to make fun of propaganda slogans and images in memes and other expressions. Also in the creative mobilization of river crabs and grass-mud horses, youth turn out to be active media producers who mobilize their "semiotic resistance" to critique official culture (Fiske 1989). Therefore, in our ethnographic work, we have tried to unpack how youth encounter, consume, and actively receive various forms of popular culture (Staiger 2005).

In analyzing such appropriations of global, regional, national, and local media cultures, we have adopted a Foucauldian approach in which power seeps through every detail of the lives of Chinese youth, and is entangled with knowledge and discourse. Chinese youth's desire for a better life are intertwined with the ideal of economic progress as advocated by the state. Power is not only exercised through control and surveillance, it has mutated and intensified in multiple domains, most prominently through the expression of individuality and the articulation of subjectivity (Foucault 1980, 1984). The desiring self is part of a complex web of power in which global capital and a socialist market economy play key roles, in conjunction with the family and the school. At certain moments, in certain places, this desiring self may upset this tightly knit web of power, may disrupt it, or even unbundle it temporarily.

Spaces constituted by popular culture and global culture in China, "real" spaces like the Internet café, and "virtual" ones like the game world, to name a few, are spaces where youth use ad hoc and loose strategies and tactics to create conditions that differ from the demands imposed upon them by the city or the factory. Fans create their own world of fandom, art village Dafen turns migrant workers into artists, and the game world turns migrant youth into virtual warriors.

Compared to their predecessors who were entrapped in the political struggle of the Cultural Revolution, impoverishment and scarcity of resources, the current generation grew up in time of progress and increased prosperity. The one child policy has nourished a generation that is more attuned to stability, an abundance of resources, for those born in the "right" place and the "right" family, and whose parents are deeply involved with their lives. Both the Internet and the influx of global culture, including brands like Apple, have triggered a culture of conspicuous consumption in the city. The discourse of the rise of

China's global power feeds into a strong nationalistic structure of feeling shared by most youth. The times have indeed changed since 1978, the year Deng Xiaoping announced his Open Door policy. However, labels such as individualism, collectivism, freedom, or democracy would not be apt to describe this generation. Nor can we say that they are part of global culture. While they are growing up in the information age like their counterparts in the West or in East Asia (see Fung 2013a; Stanat 2005), China's youth still struggle to negotiate traditional or neo-Confucian ideologies from the previous generation. Especially now that Confucianism is making a comeback in China, they are consuming predominantly information and entertainment filtered by the authorities, and grow up in a time when the difference between the rich and the poor is rapidly increasing.

In this book we have tried to steer away from using too many big words, like democracy or neoliberalism. Against all -isms mentioned in various literatures, including communism, capitalism, consumerism, cosmopolitanism, globalism, nationalism, or neoliberalism, to name the most frequently used ones, that attempt to capture the essence and process of youth development in China, we believe that singling out these big concepts does not help to capture the constantly changing youth scenes, behaviors, and cultures in contemporary China. The complexity and plurality of youth in China thus need more detailed analysis, rather than being folded into big -isms.

We have, however, not fully abandoned the -isms, and analyzed the basic layers of social structure, namely partyism, familism, and pedagogy, and identified them, in conjunction with processes of globalization and regionalization, as both limiting *and* enabling factors of youth culture. One theme that is reiterated in different chapters is the coexistence of a strong state and the fluid and ever-changing youth spaces. While in some cases, for example, young migrant workers' QQ messages have to remain hidden from the line manager, in other cases, like in Shenzhen, Dafen Art Village's painters "cling to" the local government for maintaining their shelter and residence. Youth carve out their real and virtual spaces for their identities in the context of an always present state (Clark 2012), the latter acknowledging that such youth spaces often branch out from the state's legitimized popular culture.

But there is so much more work to be done. First, our analyses inspire other questions, other inquiries, for example, more ethnography is needed to understand how popular movies like *Love Is Not Blind* are consumed by youth in their daily lives, more research is needed to understand the lives of goldfarmers, and the way their future develops, more research can give insight into the emergence of rock festivals in second and third tier cities of China. Furthermore, there are still many uncharted terrains of youth cultures that we have come across in our fieldwork in Beijing, Shanghai, Guangzhou, Hangzhou, Wuhan, and Shenzhen. What about the affluent second generation or silver spoon kids, and the *diaosi* or youthful loser, the millennium youth involved in producing *Shanzhai* cultures like fake New Year festivals, and what about rural youth, and ethnic youth? All such studies may help to multiply the idea of "China" as well as the idea of "Youth in China," and we believe this is important in order to resist any unequivocal or essentialistic narrative about China, including the trope of "the Rise of China," a trope that conveniently downplays questions like "'rise' based on which criteria?" and "whose China?".

The imagination of youth culture, mostly in the last 10 years, is only partly documented in this book and we are sure that the road ahead is even more theoretically intriguing and empirically surprising. The rapid economic development of China has accelerated the growth of youth culture to an extent that nobody could have predicted 20 years ago. Had Deng Xiaoping failed to open the door of China in the 1980s, Chinese youth might still wear the locally produced plain white shoes instead of Nike, Adidas, and New Balance every day to school. Without

China's entry into the WTO, Chinese kids could have no chance to see Disneyland in Shanghai and *Frozen* (2013) and other Hollywood movies in the cinema. Deprived of the Internet, youth might still know the world through the Party press, CCTV, and their parents. With no Facebook and Google to inspire social media like Wechat and *Baidu* in China, youth networks were still geographically bounded. All these changes happened in the recent history of China. This book might only dissect this part of history.

Youth is always also about hope, about aspiration, about a politics of possibility. As Yiu Fai Chow writes (2011: 786), "an inquiry on hope management is primarily spatial, that is focusing on the dynamics within a specific spatial context, a field or, if you like, a battlefield of hopes all striving for their own cause – and course – of life." The spaces youth carve out can also be conceived as spaces of hope, as attempts to imagine life differently and aspire for a different and hopefully better future.

In his recent book *The Future as a Cultural Fact*, Arjun Appadurai juxtaposes an ethics of probability, related to the increased rationalization and governmentalization of the state, to the ethics of possibility, which he defines as

> those ways of thinking, feeling, and acting that increase the horizons of hope, that expand the field of the imagination, that produce greater equity in what I have called the capacity to aspire, and that widen the field of informed, creative, and critical citizenship. (2013: 295)

The latter ethics inspire a politics that is geared toward the future. "We need," writes Appadurai, "to construct an understanding of the future by examining the interaction between three notable human preoccupations that shape the future as a cultural fact, that is, as a form of difference. These are imagination, anticipation, and aspiration" (2013:

286). We contend that it is in particular the new generations in China that may have the ability, mobility, and power to engage in such an ethics of possibility.

We want to end the book by translating such ethics of possibility and their related politics of hope back into history. Li Dazhao is one of the two co-founders of the Communist Party in China. After the May Fourth Movement and the subsequent failures of various attempts of many intellectuals and compatriots to reform the nation, Li turned toward communism. He met Sun Yat Sen, and participated in the Kuomintang–Communist Cooperation in 1922, but sadly, like many early martyrs, was executed by hanging under the Beiyang Government. Only later was he rehabilitated. His words echo somehow uncannily with our commitment to remain hopeful – a commitment that is naïve maybe, but that at moments strikes us as justified. For example, when we join youth during a captivating concert of Queen Sea Big Shark in Beijing's Mao bar, when we drink together till the sun rises and paints the skyline of Shanghai deep orange, when we visit the queer film festival in Beijing, when we debate the ranking of the singers in *I Am a Singer* from Hunan TV, or when they become passionate painters in Dafen Art Village.

> In youth's dictionary, there is no such word as "difficulty." In youth's saying, there is no such word as "barrier." Leaping forward, soaring up bravely, free spirited as they are. With weird and unconventional thinking, a sharp intuition, a vivid life, [youth] creates its own environment and conquers history. (Li Dazhao 1888–1927)

Or, maybe, it is fairer to give the final words in this book to today's youth, from the band Wutiaoren (5 persons), a folk band from Haifeng in Guangdong. Band member Ren Ke explained that during their days in Guangzhou, they were staying in a poor neighborhood where a lot of young people from different parts of China stayed. It was a messy, dirty, and dark place, but even there, the sun still managed to shine through on the faces of the girls, whether from Guangdong or any other province in China. This is what they express in their 2015 song titled "Guangdong Girl" (*Guangdong Guniang*):

> You say: the sun is so unusually bright today, we must dance
> But I dance messily, and it's frustrating that I keep stepping on your slippers
> Never mind, let's go out, enjoy the sun, and take a walk around the world
> Go, bring a doggy, lock the door, and leave our small room
> Dear Guangdong girl lalala
> Dear Guangdong girl I love you
> You say: it's cold in the North, it's warm in the South, the world is sometimes cold sometimes warm
> But I don't know why I don't really pay attention to what you are saying
> Dear Guangdong girl lalala
> Dear Guangdong girl I love you.

References

Abbas, A. (2008) Faking Globalization. In A. Huysen (ed.), *Other Cities, Other Worlds: Urban Imaginaries in a Globalizing Age*. Durham, NC: Duke University Press, pp. 243–64.

Anagnost, A. (2004) The Corporeal Politics of Quality (*Suzhi*). *Public Culture*, 16(2), 189–208.

Appadurai, A. (1996) *Modernity At Large: Cultural Dimensions of Globalization*. Minneapolis, MN: University of Minnesota Press.

Appadurai, A. (2013) *The Future as Cultural Fact: Essays on the Global Condition*. London: Verso.

Auge, M. (2009) *Non-Places: Introduction to an Anthropology of Supermodernity*, 2nd edn. London: Verso.

Barnard, M. (2007) *Fashion Theory: A Reader* (new edn). London and New York: Routledge.

Bauer, J., Feng, W., Riley, N. and Zhao, X. (1992) Gender Inequality in Urban China: Education and Employment. *Modern China*, 18(3), 333–70.

Beck, U. (2002) The Cosmopolitan Society and its Enemies. *Theory, Culture & Society*, 19(1–2), 17–44.

Beijing News (2016) Kong fushikang hai gongren li ai gang, tai lao tuan jiang fu gudong hui chenqing [Chinese People Love and Marriage Survey Released, "Seven Year Itch" Reduced to Five Years]. *Beijing News*, January 11. Available at: http://www.bjnews.com.cn/feature/2016/01/11/391064.html

Bijker, W. (1997) *Of Bicycles, Bakelites, and Bulbs: Toward a Theory of Sociotechnical Change*. Cambridge, MA: MIT Press.

Bourdieu, P. (2010) *Distinction*. New York: Taylor & Francis.

Brownell, S. and Wasserstrom, J. N. (2002) *Chinese Femininities/Chinese Masculinities: A Reader*. Berkeley, CA: University of California Press.

Butler, J. (1990) *Gender Trouble: Feminism and the Subversion of Identity*. London: Routledge.

Butler, J. (1993) *Bodies that Matter: On the Discursive Limits of "Sex."* New York: Routledge.

Butler, J. (1997) *Excitable Speech: A Politics of the Performative*. New York: Routledge.

Callahan, W. A. (2006) History, Identity, and Security: Producing and Consuming Nationalism in China. *Critical Asian Studies*, 38(2), 179–208.

Carah, N. (2010) *Pop Brands: Branding, Popular Music and Young People*. New York: Peter Lang.

Carey, J. (1989) *Communication as Culture*. New York: Routledge.

Chan, A. (2002) The Culture of Survival: Lives of Migrant Workers through the Prism of Private Letters. In P. Link, R. Madsen and P. Pickowicz (eds.) *Popular China: Unofficial Culture in a Globalizing Society*. New York: Rowman & Littlefield, pp. 163–88.

Chan, J. and Pun, N. (2010) Suicide as Protest for the New Generation of Chinese Migrant Workers: Foxconn, Global Capital, and the State. *Asia-Pacific Journal*, 18(2).

Chen, L. (2011) Love Is Not Blind is a Box Office Hit in China. *Asia Pacific Arts*, November 22. Available at: http://asiapacificarts.usc.edu/article@apa?love_is_not_blind_is_a_box_office_hit_in_china_17724.aspx

Chew, M. (2003) The Dual Consequences of Cultural Localization: How Exposed Short Stockings Subvert and Sustain Global Cultural Hierarchy. *Positions*, 11(2), 479–509.

Chew, M. (2007) Contemporary Re-emergence of the Qipao: Political Nationalism, Cultural Production and Popular Consumption of a Traditional Chinese Dress. *China Quarterly*, 189, 144–61.

Chow, Y. F. (2011) Hope against Hopes: Diana Zhu and the Transnational Politics of Chinese Popular Music. *Cultural Studies*, 25(6), 783–808.

Chow, Y. F. (forthcoming). Subcultures: Role of the Media. In L. van Zoonen (ed.) *International Encyclopedia of Media Studies*. Hoboken, NJ: Wiley-Blackwell.

Chow, Y. F. and de Kloet, J. (2013) *Sonic Multiplicities: Hong Kong Pop and the Global Circulation of Sound and Image*. Bristol: Intellect.

Chua, B. H. (2004) Conceptualizing an East-Asian Popular Culture. *Inter-Asia Cultural Studies*, 5(2), 200–21.

Chua, B. H. (2012) *Structure, Audience, and Soft Power in East Asian Pop Culture*. Hong Kong: Hong Kong University Press.

CIA (2016) *The World Fact Book*. Available at: https://www.cia.gov/library/publications/the-world-factbook/fields/2172.html

Civil Media Taiwan (2015) *Kong fushikang hai gongren li ai gang, tai lao tuan jiang fu gudong hui chenqing* [Accusing Foxconn of Causing Cancer to their Workers, Labour Groups from Hong Kong and Taiwan Attend Shareholders Meeting to Express their Concern]. Available at: http://www.civilmedia.tw/archives/33321

Clark, P. (2012) *Youth Culture in China: From Red Guards to Netizens*. Cambridge: Cambridge University Press.

CNNIC (2015) *China Internet Network Information Center: The 36th Statistical Report on Internet Development in China*. Available at: http://www1.cnnic.cn/IDR/

Cockain, A. (2012) *Young Chinese in Urban China*. London: Routledge.

Coleman, E. and Chou, W. (2000) *Tongzhi: Politics of Same-Sex Eroticism in Chinese Societies*. New York: Routledge.

Crane, D. (2002) Culture and Globalization: Theoretical Models and Emerging Trends. In D. Crane (ed.), *Global Culture: Media, Arts, Policy and Globalization*. London: Routledge, pp. 1–26.

Croll, E. (2013 [1978]) *Feminism and Socialism in China*. London: Routledge.

Dai, X. L. (2005) China's Unemployment Reached New High; 15 Percent Youth Aged 22 without Job. *Beijing Morning Post*, May 24. Available at: http://news.sohu.com/20050524/n225674936.shtml

de Kloet, J. (2005) Popular Music and Youth in Urban China: The Dakou Generation. *China Quarterly*, 183, 609–26.

de Kloet, J. (2008) Gendering China Studies: Peripheral Perspectives, Central Questions. *China Information*, 22(2), 195–220.

de Kloet, J. (2010) *China with a Cut: Globalisation, Urban Youth and Popular Music*. Amsterdam: Amsterdam University Press.

de Kloet, J. (2014) *Looking for a Gown: Creative Production in a Mimetic World*. Amsterdam: Amsterdam University Press.

de Kloet, J. and Scheen, L. (2013) Pudong: The Shanzhai Global City. *European Journal of Cultural Studies*, 16(6), 692–709.

de Kloet, J. and Teurlings, J. (2008) Digital Convergence Ten Years Later: Broadcast Your Selves and Web Karaoke. In J. Kooijman, P. Pisters and W. Strauven (eds.), *Mind the Screen: Media Concepts according to Thomas Elsaesser*. Amsterdam: Amsterdam University Press, pp. 345–59.

Deuze, M. (2012) *Media Life*. Cambridge: Polity.

Dillabough, J. and Kennelly, J. (2010) *Lost Youth in the Global City: Class, Culture and the Urban Imaginary*. Abingdon: Routledge.

Eglinton, K. (2012) *Understanding Youth Culture, Youth Material Consumption, and Local Places*. New York: Springer.

Engebretsen, E. L. (2015) *Queer Women in Urban China: An Ethnography*. London: Routledge.

Entwistle, J. (2000) *The Fashioned Body: Fashion, Dress and Modern Social Theory*. Cambridge: Polity.

Entwistle, J. (2009) *The Aesthetic Economy of Fashion: Markets and Values in Clothing and Modelling*. Oxford: Berg.

Evans, H. (2008) Sexed Bodies, Sexualized Identities, and the Limits of Gender. *China Information*, 22(2), 361–86.

Fan, M. and Shen, F. (2015) Daxuesheng Hunqian Xingxingwei Ji Taidu Yanjiu [Research on College Students' Premaritial Sex Behaviour and Attitude]. *Dangdai Qingnian Yanjiu*, 6, 82–7.

Farrer, J. (2002) *Opening Up: Youth Sex Culture and Market Reform in Shanghai*. Chicago, IL: University of Chicago Press.

Fincher, L. H. (2014) *Leftover Women: The Resurgence of Gender Inequality in China*. London: Zed Books.

Finnane, A. (2005) China on the Catwalk: Between Economic Success and National Anxiety. *China Quarterly*, 183, 587–608.

Fiske, J. (1989) *Understanding Popular Culture*. New York: Routledge.

Foucault, M. (1978) *The History of Sexuality: An Introduction*. New York: Vintage Books.

Foucault, M. (1980) *Power/Knowledge: Selected Interviews and Other Writings, 1972–1977*, ed. C. Gordon. New York: Pantheon Books.

Foucault, M. (1981) Omnes et Singulatim: Towards a Criticism of "Political Reason." In S. McMurrin (ed.), *The Tanner Lectures on Human Values, vol. 2*. Salt Lake City, UT: University of Utah Press, pp. 223–54.

Foucault, M. (1984) What is Enlightenment? In P. Rabinow (ed.) *Foucault Reader*. New York: Pantheon, pp. 32–50.

Foucault, M. (1990) *The History of Sexuality, Vol. 2: The Use of Pleasure*, trans. R. Hurley (reissue edn). New York: Vintage Books.

Foucault, M. (2000) The Subject and Power. In P. Rabinow (ed.), *Power* (Vol. 3). New York: New Press, pp. 326–48.

Foucault, M., Ewald, F., Fontana, A. and Davidson, A. I. (2007) *Security, Territory, Population: Lectures at the Collège de France 1977–1978*, ed. M. Senellart, trans. G. Burchell. London: Picador.

Fung, A. (2007) Intra-Asian Cultural Flow: Cultural Homologies in Hong Kong and Japanese Television Soap Operas. *Journal of Broadcasting and Electronic Media*, 51(2), 265–86.

Fung, A. (2008a) Western Style, Chinese Pop: Jay Chou's Rap and Hip-Hop in China. *Asian Music*, 39(1), 69–80.

Fung, A. (2008b) Media Consumption and Incomplete Globalization: How Chinese Interpret Border-Crossing Hong Kong TV Dramas. In Y. Kim (ed.), *Media Consumption and Everyday Life in Asia*. London: Routledge, pp. 83–96.

Fung, A. (2010) Harmonizing the Global Recession in China. *Popular Communication*, 8(3), 169–74.

Fung, A. (ed.) (2013a) *Asian Popular Culture: The Global (Dis)continuity*. New York: Routledge.

Fung, A. (2013b) Deliberating Fandom and New Wave of Chinese Pop: A Case Study of Chris Li. *Popular Music*, 32, 79–89.

Fung, A. (forthcoming) *Global Game Industries and Cultural Policy*. London: Palgrave Macmillan.

Fung, A. and Choe, K. (2013) Affect in TV Drama: A Comparison between the Korean and Chinese Version of *Meteor Shower*. *Journal of Korean Studies*, 161, 363–99 (in Korean).

Gang G. (2005) Party Recruitment of College Students in China. *Journal of Contemporary China*, 14(43), 371–93.

Gao, H. and Li, Q. (2011) "Defeminization" of Women Village Leaders: Sex, Gender and Leadership. *Collection of Women's Studies*. Available at: http://en.cnki.com.cn/Article_en/CJFDTOTAL-FNYJ201101006.htm

García-Canclini, N. (1995) *Consumidores y ciudadanos: Conflictos multiculturales de la globalización* [*Consumers and Citizens: Globalization and Multicultural Conflicts*]. Mexico: Grijalbo.

Geyer, R. (2002) In Love and Gay. In P. Link, R. Madsen and P. Pickowicz (eds.) *Popular China: Unofficial Culture in a Globalizing Society*. New York: Rowman & Littlefield, pp. 251–74.

Giddens, A. (1982) *The Consequences of Modernity*. Stanford, CA: Stanford University Press.

Global Times (2014) If You Are the Foreign One | Target Chinese. *Global Times*, December 21. Available at: http://language.globaltimes.cn/if-you-are-the-foreign-one/#.Ve3C1nsUz_5

Gov.cn (2007) Shiliu da yilai dangyuan duiwu buduan gaishan dangyuan yi da 7336.3 Wan [Since the 16th Party Congress, Party Membership Continues to Improve to 73.3 million]. Available at: http://www.gov.cn/ztzl/17da/content_770731.htm

Gries, P. (2004) *China's New Nationalism: Pride, Politics, and Diplomacy*. Berkeley, CA: University of California Press.

Groenewegen-Lau, J. (2011) Asima, her Pimp and a Melancholic Boss. *Norient*, May 4. Available at: http://norient.com/academic/groenewegen2011/

Groenewegen-Lau, J. (2014) Steel and Strawberries: How Chinese Rock Became State-Sponsored. *Asian Music*, 45(1), 3–33.

Gross, D. (1982) Time–Space Relations in Giddens' Social Theory. *Theory, Culture & Society*, 1(2), 83–8.

Grossberg, L. (2010) *Cultural Studies in the Future Tense*. Durham, NC: Duke University Press.

Gui, Y., Berry, J. W. and Zheng, Y. (2012) Migrant Worker Acculturation in China. *International Journal of Intercultural Relations*, 36(4), 598–610.

Guo, K. and Wu, Y. (2009) *Woguo Chengshi Qingshaonian De Meijie Xiaofei Yu Quanqiuguan* [City Teenagers' Media Consumption and Global Values]. *Xinwen Daxue*, 3, 114–37.

Han Han (2012) *This Generation: Dispatches from China's Most Popular Blogger*. London: Simon & Schuster.

Hays, J. (2015) Facts and Details: Migrant Workers in China. Available at: http://factsanddetails.com/china/cat11/sub72/item150.html

Hebdige, D. (1979) *Subculture: The Meaning of Style*. London: Methuen.

Hine, C. (2015) *Ethnography for the Internet: Embedded, Embodied and Everyday*. London: Bloomsbury Academic.

Hinsch, B. (1990) *Passions of the Cut Sleeve: The Male Homosexual Tradition in China*. Berkeley, CA: University of California Press.

Hong Kong Liberal Studies Association (n.d.). Contemporary Chinese Family Structure and Changes of Family Relationship. Available at: http://www.hklsa.org.hk/upload/chapter/original/075847438208.doc (in Chinese).

Huang, H. (2012) Breaking the Mold. *WWD: Women's Wear Daily*, 203(116), 8-1.

Huang, Y. and Pan, S. (2012) Zhongguo Shaonan Shaonv De Ai Yu Xing – Jiyu 2010 Nian 14–17 Sui Quanguo Zong Renkou De Suiji Chouyang Diaocha [Love and Sex of Chinese Boys and Girls – Based on a Random Sampling Survey of National Population Aged from 14 to 17 in 2010]. *Zhongguo Qingnian Yanjiu*, 7, 55–61.

Hub (2015) 10 K-Pop Korean Boy Bands You Should Know. Hub, July 30. Available at: http://hubpages.com/technology/5-K-Pop-Korean-Boy-Bands -You-Should-Know.

Illouz, E. (2007) *Cold Intimacies: The Making of Emotional Capitalism*. Cambridge: Polity.

Inglehart, R. (1977) *The Silent Revolution: Changing Values and Political Styles among Western Publics*. Princeton, NJ: Princeton University Press.

Jacobs, K. (2012) *People's Pornography: Sex and Surveillance on the Chinese Internet*. Chicago, IL: University of Chicago Press.

Jacobs, K. (2015) *The Afterglow of Women's Pornography in Post-Digital China*. New York: Palgrave Macmillan.

Jankowiak, W. (2013) Chinese Youth: Hot Romance and Cold Calculation. In P. Link, R. P. Madsen and P. G. Pickowicz (eds.), *Restless China*. Lanham, MD: Rowman & Littlefield, pp. 189–210.

Jeffreys, E. and Sigley, G. (2009) Governmentality, Governance, and China. In E. Jeffreys (ed.), *China's Governmentalities: Governing Change, Changing Government*. London: Routledge, pp. 1–23.

Jenkins, H. (2006) *Convergence Culture: Where Old and New Media Collide.* New York: New York University Press.

Jun, S. X. (2008) *Unhappy China.* Nanjing: Phoenix Media Publishing Group.

Jurriëns, E. and de Kloet, J. (2007) *Cosmopatriots: On Distant Belongings and Close Encounters.* Amsterdam: Rodopi.

Kaiser, S. (2013) *Fashion and Cultural Studies.* London: Bloomsbury Academic.

Kam, L. (2013) *Shanghai Lalas: Female Tongzhi Communities and Politics in Urban China.* Hong Kong: Hong Kong University Press.

Keane, M. (2013) *Creative Industries in China: Art, Design and Media.* Cambridge: Polity.

Keane, M., Fung, A. and Moran, A. (2007) *New Television Globalization and East Asian Cultural Imaginations.* Hong Kong: Hong Kong University Press.

Kipnis, A. (2012) *Chinese Modernity and the Individual Pysche.* London: Palgrave Macmillan.

Kong, S. Y. (2013) *Are You the One?*: The Competing Public Voices of China's Post-1980s Generation. In P. Link, R. P. Madsen and P. G. Pickowicz (eds.), *Restless China.* Lanham, MD: Rowman & Littlefield, pp. 127–48.

Kong, T. S. K. (2010) *Chinese Male Homosexualities: Memba, Tongzhi and Golden Boy.* New York: Routledge.

Kuipers, G. (2014) In Praise of Doubt: Academic Virtues, Transnational Encounters and the Problem of the Public. *European Journal of Cultural Studies,* 17, 75–89.

Laqueur, W. (1956) *Communism and Nationalism in the Middle East.* London: Routledge & Kegan Paul.

Latour, B. (1987) *Science in Action.* Cambridge, MA: Harvard University Press.

Lau, J. (2016) The Role of Media in Constructing the Power Relation between Class: A Comparison between Chinese and Korean Versions of *Running Man.* Unpublished thesis, School of Journalism and Communication, Chinese University of Hong Kong.

Lazzarato, M. (1996) Immaterial Labour. In P. Virno and M. Hardt (eds.), *Radical Thought in Italy: A Potential Politics.* Minneapolis, MN: University of Minnesota Press, pp. 132–46.

Lemke, T. (2002) Foucault, Governmentality and Critique. *Rethinking Marxism,* 14(3), 49–64.

Leung, H. H.-S. (2008) *Undercurrents: Queer Culture and Postcolonial Hong Kong.* Vancouver: University of British Columbia Press.

Li, C. (2013) Impact of Beauty Fashion on Contemporary Chinese Youth. *Canadian Social Science,* 9(6), 15–20.

Li, C. (2015) Jingqiaoqiao De Geming Shifou Linjin? – Cong 80hou He 90hou De Jiazhiguan Zhuanbian Kan Nianqing Yidai De Xianxingxing [Is the Silent

Revolution Coming? A Discussion about Young Generation's Advancement according to the Change of "80hou"'s and "90hou"'s Values]. *Hebei Xuejan*, 3, 100–4.

Li, D. (2015) "Ordinary People" are Added in the Third Season of *Running Man*. When it is Rebroadcast is Still Unknown. *Liaoning Channel*, October 29. Available at: http://liaoning.nen.com.cn/system/2015/10/29/018568255.shtml

Li, H. B. (2007) 人民時評：重新認識' 工人' – 中國工會新聞 – 人民網 [Comments from *People's Daily*: Knowing "Workers" Once More]. *People's Daily Online*, April 30. Available at: http://acftu.people.com.cn/BIG5/5688786.html

Li, Y. and Niu, X. (2008) Daxuesheng Xingzhishi Laiyuan He Xingjiaoyu Xuqiu De Diaocha Yu Fenxi [Investigation and Analysis of College Students' Sex Knowledge Source and Sex Education Need]. *Zhongguo Xing Kexue*, 17(7), 7–8.

Liang, X. S. (2012) *Analysis of China's Social Differentiation*. Hong Kong: Joint Publishing (in Chinese).

Lim, S. (2006) *Celluloid Comrades: Representations of Male Homosexuality in Contemporary Chinese Cinemas*. Honolulu, HI: University of Hawaii Press.

Lin, J. (2008) "80hou" Daxuesheng Sixiang Tedian De Diaocha Yu Fenxi [Investigation and Analysis of "80hou" College Students' Ideological Characteristics]. *Qinzhou Xueyuan Xuebao*, 23(5), 83–6.

Lin, L. and Chen, C. (2016) China's Censors Take Another Gay-Themed Web Drama Offline. *Wall Street Journal*, February 24. Available at: http://blogs.wsj.com/chinarealtime/2016/02/24/chinas-censors-take-another-gay-themed-web-drama-offline/

Lin, Z. and Fung, A. (2013) The Myth of "Shanzhai" Culture and the Paradox of Digital Democracy in China. *Inter-Asia Cultural Studies*, 14(3), 401–16.

Link, P. and Qiang, W. (2013) From Grass-Mud Equestrians to Rights-Conscious Citizens: Language and Thought on the Chinese Internet. In P. Link, R. P. Madsen and P. G. Pickowicz (eds.), *Restless China*. Lanham, MD: Rowman & Littlefield, pp. 83–106.

Liu, F. (2013) *Urban Youth in China: Modernity, the Internet and the Self*. London: Routledge.

Lu, H. (2013) Communist Youth League Convenes National Congress, *Xinhuanet*, June 17. Available at: http://news.xinhuanet.com/english/china/2013-06/17/c_132461856.htm

Lu, J. and Wang, X. (2013) 20 Shiji 90 Niandai Yilai Woguo Hunyin Zhuangkuang Bianhua Fenxi [An Analysis of Chinese Marriage Situation Changes from 1990s]. *Beijing Shehui Kexue*, 3, 62–72.

Lu, Q. and Che, Y. (2009) Daxue Xinsheng Xing Guannian Diaocha Ji Jiaoyu Sikao [Investigation of College Freshmen's Sex Attitude and Related Education Reflection]. *Zhongguo Xing Kexue*, 4, 43–6.

Luo, W. and Sun, Z. (2014) Are You the One? China's TV Dating Shows and the Sheng Nü's Predicament. *Feminist Media Studies*, 1–18.

Ma, K. (2011) Love is Not Blind. Review. Available at: http://www.lovehkfilm.com/reviews_2/love_is_not_blind.html

Maira, S. and Soep, E. (2004) *Youthscapes: The Popular, the National, the Global*. Philadelphia, PA: University of Pennsylvania Press.

Mannheim, K. (1952) *Essays in the Sociology of Knowledge*. London: Robert Kennedy Publishing.

McClary, S. and Walser, R. (1990) Start Making Sense! Musicology Wrestles with Rock. In S. Firth and A. Goodwin (eds.), *On Record: Rock, Pop, and the Written Word*. London: Routledge, pp. 277–92.

Meng, B. (2009) Who Needs Democracy If We Can Pick Our Favourite Girl? Super Girl as Media Spectacle. *Chinese Journal of Communication*, 2, 257–72.

Meng, B. (2011) From Steamed Bun to Grass-Mud Horse: E Gao as Alternative Political Discourse on the Chinese Internet. *Global Media and Communication*, 7(1), 33–51.

Moran, A. (1998) *Copycat Television: Globalisation, Program Formats and Cultural Identity*. Luton: University of Luton Press.

Morris, M. (1988) Banality in Cultural Studies. *Discourse*, 10, 3–29.

Naftali, O. (2014) *Children, Right and Modernity in China: Raising Self-Governing Citizens*. London: Palgrave Macmillan.

Nealon, J. (2008) *Foucault Beyond Foucault: Power and its Intensifications since 1984*. Stanford, CA: Stanford University Press.

Nyíri, P., Zhang, J. and Varrall, M. (2010). China's Cosmopolitan Nationalists: "Heroes" and "Traitors" of the 2008 Olympics. *The China Journal*, 63, 25–55.

Ong, A. (2006) *Neoliberalism as Exception, Exception to Neoliberalism*. Durham, NC: Duke University Press.

Osgerby, B. (2004) *Youth Media*. London: Routledge.

Pang, L. (2012) *Creativity and its Discontents: China's Creative Industries and Intellectual Property Rights Offenses*. Durham, NC: Duke University Press.

Peng, M. (2016) Wode 17 Ge Ji You Gaosu Ni GAY Quan "You Duo Luan" [My 17 Gay Friends]. Available at: http://dwz.cn/2FsLDv

Pi, C. (2016) *Producing the Daring and Desiring Self in the Love Club in Shanghai*. Unpublished manuscript under review.

Poell, T., de Kloet, J. and Zeng, G. (2014) Will the Real Weibo Please Stand Up? Chinese Online Contention and Actor-Network Theory. *Chinese Journal of Communication*, 7(1), 1–18.

Postiglione, G. (2011) Education. In X. Zang (ed.), *Understanding Chinese Society*. Abingdon: Routledge, pp. 80–95.

Price, R. F. (1970) *Education in Communist China*. London: Routledge & Kegan Paul.

Pun, N. (2003) Subsumption or Consumption? The Phantom of Consumer Revolution in "Globalizing" China. *Cultural Anthropology*, 18(4), 469–92.

Pun, N. (2005) *Made in China: Women Factory Workers in a Global Workplace*. Durham, NC: Duke University Press.

Qiu, J. L., Cartier, C. and Castells, M. (2009) *Working-Class Network Society: Communication Technology and the Information Have-Less in Urban China*. Cambridge, MA: MIT Press.

Quandl (2014) China Population Overview. Available at: https://www.quandl.com/collections/china/china-population

Rea, C. (2013) Spoofing (e'gao) Culture on the Chinese Internet. In J. Milner Davis and J. Chey (eds.), *Humour in Chinese Life and Culture: Resistance and Control in Modern Times*. Hong Kong: Hong Kong University Press, pp. 149–72.

Ren, M. (2003) Sociological Analysis of the Phenomenon of Alienation of Youth Culture. *Contemporary Youth Studies*, 1, 21–4.

Renminwang (2015) *Zhongguo gongchandang dangyuan da 8779.3 Wan* [Chinese Party Membership Reaches 87,793,000]. Available at: http://society.people.com.cn/n/2015/0630/c136657-27227285.html

Rofel, L. (2007) *Desiring China: Experiments in Neoliberalism, Sexuality, and Public Culture*. Durham, NC: Duke University Press.

Rosen, S. (2009) Contemporary Chinese Youth and the State. *Journal of Asian Studies*, 68(2), 359–69.

Rosen, S. (2015) Hollywood in China: Selling Out or Cashing In? *The Diplomat*, May 26. Available at: http://thediplomat.com/2015/05/hollywood-in-china-selling-out-or-cashing-in/

Ruan, P., Huang, Y. and Wu, P. (2011) 80hou Daxue Biyesheng Xingshenghuo Fangshi Diaocha Yanjiu [Investigation of "80hou" College Graduates' Sex Behaviour]. *Zhongguo Jiankang Xinlixue Zazhi*, 19(2), 214–17.

Sardar, Z. (2000) *The Consumption of Kuala Lumpur*. London: Reaktion Books.

Scheen, L. (2015) *Shanghai Literary Imaginings: A City in Transformation*. Amsterdam: Amsterdam University Press.

Sharma, Y. (2014) What Do You Do with Millions of Extra Graduates? BBC Business, July 1. Available at: http://www.bbc.com/news/business-28062071

Shen, H. and Wang, L. (eds.) (2012) *90hou De Shuzi Shenghuo: 90hou Daxuesheng Yanjiu Baogao* [The Digital Life of those Born in the 90s: The Research Report of College Students Born in the 90s]. Beijing: Jixie Gongye Chubanshe.

Shi, T. (2015) *The Cultural Logic of Politics in Mainland China and Taiwan*. New York: Cambridge University Press.

Shi, Z. (ed.) (2013) *Dangdai Daxuesheng Sixiang Tedian Yu Fazhan Qushi Diaoyan Baogao*. [Investigation Report of Contemporary College Students' Thinking Characteristics and Development Trend]. Beijing: Qinghua Chubanshe.

Shifman, L. (2011) An Anatomy of a YouTube Meme. *New Media & Society*, 14(2), 187–203.

Shih, S.-M. (2013) Comparison as Relation. In R. Felski and S. Stanford (eds.), *Comparison: Theories, Approaches, Uses*. Baltimore, MD: Johns Hopkins University Press, pp. 79–98.

Shohat, E. and Stam, R. (1994) *Unthinking Eurocentrism: Multiculturalism and the Media*. London: Routledge.

Staiger, J. (2005) *Media Reception Studies*. New York: New York University Press.

Stanat, M. (2005) *China's Generation Y: Understanding the Future Leader of the World's Next Superpower*. Paramus, NJ: Homa & Sekey Books.

Steele, V. (2010) *The Berg Companion to Fashion*. Oxford: Berg.

Stephenson, W. (1988) *The Play Theory of Mass Communication*. New Brunswick, NJ: Transaction Publishers.

Stockmann, D. and Gallagher, M. E. (2011) Remote Control: How the Media Sustain Authoritarian Rule in China. *Comparative Political Studies*, 44(4), 436–67.

Sun, W. (2009) *Maid in China: Media, Morality, and the Cultural Politics of Boundaries*. London and New York: Routledge.

Sun, W. (2010) Narrating Translocality: Dagong Poetry and the Subaltern Imagination. *Mobilities*, 5(3), 291–309.

Sun, W. (2012) The Poetry of Spiritual Homelessness: A Creative Practice of Coping with Industrial Alienation. In A. Kipnis (ed.), *Chinese Modernity and the Individual Psyche*. London: Palgrave Macmillan, pp. 67–85.

Sun, W. (2013) The Cultural Politics of Recognition: Rural Migrants and Documentary Films in China. *Journal of Chinese Cinemas*, 7(1), 3–20.

Sun, W. (2014) *If You Are the One*: Dating Shows, Reality TV, and the Politics of the Personal in Urban China. *Australian Review of Public Affairs*, October. Available at: http://www.australianreview.net/digest/2014/10/sun.html

Tao, M. Y. (2014) Foreign Media: Emerging Trends about Youth of Chinese Characteristics Facing Danger of Unemployment. *Tencent Finance*, February 21. Available at: http://finance.qq.com/a/20140221/016123.htm

Taussig, M. (1993) *Mimesis and Alterity: A Particular History of the Senses*. New York: Routledge.

Tomlinson, J. (1999) *Globalization and Culture*. Hoboken, NJ: John Wiley & Sons.

Tsang, M. C. (1996) Financial Reform of Basic Education in China. *Economics of Education Review*, 15(4), 423–44.

Turner, Y. and Acker, A. (2002) *Education in New China*. Farnham: Ashgate.

van Dijck, J. (2013) *The Culture of Connectivity: A Critical History of Social Media*. Oxford: Oxford University Press.

Wagner, K., Yu, T. and Vulpiani, L. (2014) Introduction: China's iGeneration. In M. Johnston, K. Wagner, T. Yu and L. Vulpiani (eds.), *China's iGeneration*. New York: Bloomsbury Academic, pp. 1–22.

Wallis, C. (2013) *Technomobility in China: Young Migrant Women and Mobile Phones*. New York: New York University Press.

Wang, B., Li, X., Stanton, B., Kamali, V., Naar-King, S., Shah, I. and Thomas, R. (2007) Sexual Attitudes, Pattern of Communication, and Sexual Behaviour among Unmarried Out-of-School Youth in China. *BMC Public Health*, 7, 189.

Wang, J. (1996) *High Culture Fever: Politics, Aesthetics, and Ideology in Deng's China*. Berkeley, CA: University of California Press.

Wang, Y. (2015) Violence, Wuxia, Migrants: Jia Zhangke's Cinematic Discontent in *A Touch of Sin*. *Journal of Chinese Cinemas*, 9(2), 159–72.

Wang, Y. S. (2006) Analysis of Change of Family Structure in Contemporary China I. *Social Science in China* 1, 96–108 (in Chinese).

Wang, Z. (2015) *Shouji Wangluo Dui Qingshaonian Shenghuo Fangshi De Yingxiang Yanjiu – Jiyu Zhejiangsheng 2384 Fen Wenjuan De Fenxi* [Mobile Phone Network's Influence on Teenagers' Lifestyle – Based on 2384 Participants in Zhejiang Province]. Master's thesis, Hangzhou Shifan Daxue.

Warikoo, N. (2014) *Balancing Acts: Youth in the Global City*. Berkeley, CA: University of California. Press.

Watson, R. and Ebrey, P. (1991) *Marriage and Inequality in Chinese Society*. Berkeley, CA: University of California Press.

Wei, T. (2015) Voices from Asian Feminist Activism: A Look at the Beijing Conference through Lesbian Eyes. *Asian Journal of Women's Studies*, 21(3), 316–25.

Wei, W. (2007) "Wandering Men" No Longer Wander Around: The Production and Transformation of Local Homosexual Identities in Contemporary Chengdu, China. *Inter-Asia Cultural Studies*, 8(4), 572–88.

Wen, C. (2010) For Love or Money. *China Daily*, April 8. Available at: http://www.chinadaily.com.cn/cndy/2010-08/04/content_11091992.htm

Wikipedia (2015) List of Countries by Internet Connection Speeds. Available at: https://en.wikipedia.org/wiki/List_of_countries_by_Internet_connection_speeds

Williams, G. A. (2015) *Fashion China*. London: Thames & Hudson.

Williams, R. (2003) *Television: Technology and Cultural Form*. London: Routledge.

Wong, D. (2015) Sexuality in China's Sexual Revolution: Asexual Marriage as Coping Strategy. *Sexualities*, 18(1–2), 100–16.

Wong, W. W. Y. (2013) *Van Gogh on Demand: China and the Readymade*. Chicago, IL: University of Chicago Press.

Xinhua (2007) China's Communist Youth League has 73.496 Million Members. *China Daily*, May 4. Available at: http://www.chinadaily.com.cn/china/2007-05/04/content_865669.htm

Xinhua (2013) 全国妇联:中国农村留守儿童数量超6000万 – 新华时政 – 新华网 [All-China Women's Federation: Left-Behind Children in China's Rural Area Exceed 60 Million]. *Xinhua*, October 5. Available at: http://news.xinhuanet.com/politics/2013-05/10/c_115720450.htm

Xu, L. (2002) *Searching for Life's Meaning: Changes and Tensions in the Worldviews of Chinese Youth in the 1980s*. Ann Arbor, MI: University of Michigan Press.

Yang, C. Z. and Zhang S. J. (2005) A Preface to China's Youth Popular Cultural Phenomenon Report. People.com.cn, August 10. Available at: http://theory.people.com.cn/BIG5/41038/3606615.html.

Yang, G. (2011) *The Power of the Internet in China: Citizen Activism Online* (reprint edn). New York: Columbia University Press.

Yang, J. R. (2015) 抗議血汗鴻海 富士康工人患白血病 勞團裸體快閃抗議 | 公民行動影音紀錄資料庫 [Protesting Blood-Sweating Hon Hai, Foxconn Workers Suffering Leukaemia; Worker's Solidarity's Naked Demonstration and Flash Mob]. Civil Media Taiwan, June 23. Available at: http://www.civilmedia.tw/archives/33277

Yang, X. (2010) China Curbs "Vulgar" Reality TV Show. *New York Times*, July 18. Available at: http://www.nytimes.com/2010/07/19/world/asia/19chinatv.html

Yiguanzhiku and Tengxun QQ (2014) *Zhongguo 90hou Qingnian Diaocha Baogao 2014* [China "90hou" Youth Survey Report 2014]. Beijing: Enfodesk.

Youku (2015) *Zhanghuimei 2015 nian 10 yue 11 ri wutuobang beijing-caihong* [A-Mei, October 11, 2015: Utopia Beijing Rainbow]. Available at: http://www.youkuinfo.com/video/224224/20151011-

Yuan, Y. and Zhang, J. (eds.) (2011) *Women, 90hou!* [We, 90hou!]. Hangzhou: Zhejiang Daxue Chubanshe.

Yue, X. D. (2007) *Idolatry and Fans: Analysis of Youth's Idol Worship*. Hong Kong: City University Press (in Chinese).

Zhang, Q. (2015) Sexuality and the Official Construction of Occidentalism in Maoist and Early Post-Mao China. *European Journal of Cultural Studies*, 18(1), 86–107.

Zhang, X. (2014) Satellite TV Will Produce 200 Reality Shows Next Year. *Xinhuanet*, November 20. Available at: http://www.hb.xinhuanet.com/2014 -11/20/c_1113326075_2.htm

Zhang Z. (2000) Mediating Time: The "Rice Bowl of Youth" in Fin de Siècle Urban China. *Public Culture*, 12(1), 93–113.

Zhao, Y. (2009) *Catching Up or Leading the Way: American Education in the Age of Globalization*. Alexandria, VA: ASCD.

Zhong, X. (2006) Who is a Feminist? Understanding the Ambivalence towards Shanghai Baby, "Body Writing" and Feminism in Post-Women's Liberation China. *Gender & History*, 18(3), 635–60.

Zhonghua Renmin Gongheguo Guojia Tongjiju (2011a), *2010 Nian Diliuci Quanguo Renkou Pucha Zhuyao Shuju Gongbao (Diyihao)* [The Report on Main Data of the Sixth National Population Census in 2010 (No. 1)]. Available at: http://www.stats.gov.cn/tjsj/tjgb/rkpcgb/qgrkpcgb/201104/ t20110428_30327.html

Zhonghua Renmin Gongheguo Guojia Tongjiju (2011b) *2010 Nian Diliuci Quanguo Renkou Pucha Zhuyao Shuju Gongbao (Diyihao)* [The Report on Main Data of the Sixth National Population Census in 2010 (No. 2)]. Available at: http://www.stats.gov.cn/tjsj/tjgb/rkpcgb/qgrkpcgb/201104/ t20110429_30328.html

Zou, Q. (2011) *80 hou daxuesheng yu 90 hou daxuesheng jiazhiguan bijiao fenxi – jiyu tongyifen diaocha wenjuan de liangci diaocha jieguo* [A Comparison Analysis between "80s" College Students' Values and "90s" College Students' Values – Based on Two Results from a Similar Questionnaire]. *Guanxi Jiaoyuxueyuan Xuebao*, 3: 71–75.

Zurndorfer, H. (2016) Men, Women, Money, and Morality: The Development of China's Sexual Economy. *Feminist Economics*, 22(2), 1–23.

Index